About the Author

Anthony Centore Ph.D. is Founder and CEO of Thriveworks (a chain of 30+ counseling centers), Private Practice Consultant for the 50,000+ member American Counseling Association, and Columnist for Counseling Today magazine. Anthony is a Licensed Counselor in Massachusetts, Virginia, Georgia, and Colorado, and has been featured on CBS Sunday Morning, ABC news, Entrepreneur, The Boston Globe, Chicago Tribune, The Washington Post, and other local and national publications. Find him online @anthonycentore.

Ask A Question!

Have a question about the content in this book, or another practice-related issue?

Go ahead and ask! Find us on twitter @thriveworks or @anthonycentore.

TABLE OF CONTENT

101: Planning a Private Practice

Lesson 1:
An Introduction That Won't Bore You

As counselors, when we venture into private practice for the first time, we make the difficult transition from technician to entrepreneur. The immensity of this transition cannot be overstated.

As technicians, we are responsible for our craft—professional counseling. As entrepreneurs, we oversee a much broader spectrum of responsibilities. The change is the equivalent to a pizza dough thrower deciding to open a restaurant. During this transition, many counselors make a fatal error: they assume that running a practice is mostly about doing counseling.

It's not.

To many in our industry, that statement is blasphemy. Our care-focused culture tells us that to turn our attention to "business" is to undermine client care. In that vein, many of us are taught that if we provide really good clinical care, the business will grow around us as our just reward.

It won't.

I have seen good clinicians fail because of poor practice management. Scheduling errors, billing errors, cash-flow problems, unreturned voicemails, unkempt offices, unfulfilled records requests, poor customer service, unsuccessful advertising spends—all of these contribute to a practice's demise.

While good counseling alone won't make a practice successful, a well-run practice is best positioned to offer great clinical care, customer service and support, and a consistent quality experience that exceeds client expectations.

This is easier said than done. As practice owner, you may be a "one man" clinical staff, as well as CEO, CFO, CMO, CSO, CTO, COO, and receptionist! How do you manage all these roles with excellence?

Lesson 2:
The Question: Should I Start a Private Practice?

I often talk about the benefits of starting a private practice. However, owning your own business isn't for everyone, and working for a counseling agency is not an inferior alternative. Listed below are 4 reasons to not start a private practice. If any one of the following applies to you, starting a practice may be a bad fit.

1) I need money now!

I have stated that a licensed counselor can start a practice for as little as a few thousand dollars, and that the practice could become cash flow positive within a few months. This is still true. However, one shouldn't expect to bring in much net profit in year one. Hence, if you are undercapitalized or need a fulltime income right away, starting a practice might not be the best career choice.

2) I want to keep my work separate from my life!

Due to the nature of the job, counselors often struggle with leaving their work at the office; if you own the office, multiply that struggle by 10. For the small business owner, work is intertwined with life. It's like having a child: the business requires constant attention. You will be home with it on Friday nights. You will be up at 4am comforting and feeding your business.

3) I hate business! / I just want to be a counselor!

Running a private practice has little to do with counseling and a lot to do with operations (billing, staffing, administration, etc.). I have never met a successful private practice owner who dislikes business. If you're starting your practice longing for the day that you can focus exclusively on client care, you should think about joining an agency.

4) I don't want to start from scratch!

When starting a practice, often both the business and the clinician are starting from scratch. Get prepared to enter a whole new world of learning. Successful practice owners have read a library's worth of business books, and have aggressively sought information and mentorship. In addition, building a company is a gauntlet of successes and failures. If you're not interested in getting an MBA from the School of Hard Knocks, think agency.

Becoming a High Paid Agency Employee

Some counselors think about working for a counseling agency as a "pay me a wage, and I'll come to work" situation. In contrast, to become a high paid agency employee, it's better think about agency work as a partnership where both parties bring value to the table. Traditionally, an agency provides office space, clients, clinical supervision, insurance, branding, and a variety of administrative services in exchange for a share of the money a clinician's services produce. This is the case regardless of whether one is paid hourly, salary, or a percentage of counseling fees.

Hence, to become a high paid agency employee, a clinician needs to bring more to the table. For example, counselors become more valuable to agencies when they:

1) Get the word out about their services instead of asking the agency to market their services for them.

2) Speak publically, and mention the agency.

3) Speak with reporters to get quoted in print, or on the news (especially if they use the agency's name).

4) Publish, tweet, and build an online or offline audience.

5) Build a reputation that brings in more clients. This is especially true if their reputation also brings in clients for other providers at the agency!

6) Offer specialized services. This is valuable to the extent that their presence allows the practice to accept clients they would otherwise need to refer (e.g., children, foreign language speaking, autism).

7) Self-manage, or request less administrative support from the agency.

8) Provide supervision or help to other providers at the agency.

9) Are credentialed with various insurance companies (note: some agencies now require clinicians to be on insurance panels to even apply for a position).

Done right, one might find that working for an agency affords more freedom, and sometimes more money, than private practice. Finally, if you're bringing serious value to the table, and your agency isn't recognizing it, it might be time to look for a practice that will!

Lesson 3:
Bootstrapping: Getting Started with Empty Pockets

One great thing about being a counselor is there are so many places to perform the trade. One can work for schools, insurance companies, employee assistance programs, group practices/agencies, nonprofits, residential care, government-funded programs and clinics, and many others. Although the employment landscape is diverse, many counselors begin their careers with the dream of someday having their very own private practice. To be their own boss! To steer their own ship! This lesson is for those counselors.

In the paragraphs that follow, we will look at eight fundamental disciplines for striking out on your own. The approach is that of the "bootstrapper." It requires little financial capital but lots of sweat equity.

1) Make the commitment

Ambivalence is the enemy of change, and when it comes to starting a practice, many counselors have it in surplus. This is understandable! Counselors often work multiple jobs — full time for the school system, part time doing in-home therapy and then top off the week with a few hours of supervision. Even when these jobs aren't one's ideal, they can provide enough to keep a person questioning whether he or she should leave well enough alone. Add to this financial pressures. I often hear providers say, "I'd rather work for myself, but my job with the university means my daughter will get free tuition" or "I'm not financially secure enough that I can give up my salary."

These are real dilemmas. However, most counselors don't need to quit their day jobs if they can find a few additional hours each week to direct toward their practices. For those with no room in their schedules, they may be wise to determine that starting a private practice isn't right for them.

Whatever the decision, bootstrappers know whether they're in or they're out. If they're in, they're committed to the challenge.

2) Pay the price

An ancient proverb translates, "Make your choice and pay the price." Indeed, there is a cost to starting a private practice. For the bootstrapper, that cost is time! Are you ready to quit book club, the bowling league, the band, and to cancel cable and box up the Xbox? You're going to need those hours.

When starting a business, life as you know it will consist of work, family time, exercise and building your practice. That's it! Make another pot of coffee and get ready for some late nights. Get ready for early mornings, too. You'll know you're on the right track when you can greet the entire 5 a.m. McDonald's staff by name.

Want to know what you'll be doing during these long hours? Skip to the later lesson, "Building a full caseload of counseling clients."

3) Focus

Because your time will be limited, you will need to be extremely focused. This means nothing can interfere with bootstrapping time: no e-mails, no phone calls, nothing that doesn't directly relate to moving the business forward. My wife Ellen is currently in her second year at law school. Being a wife and a mother (and an adjunct professor), she has a fraction of the time her classmates do to study. However, she still makes the dean's list! This isn't just because she's brilliant. It's because when Ellen studies — from noon to 3 p.m. every weekday — she's super focused. In contrast, her classmates have their books open all the time, sometimes camping out at the law school, but they waste huge swaths of time with unfocused study habits. Ellen, like the bootstrapper, knows that the power of focus cannot be overstated.

4) Pursue constant forward motion

When I built Thrive Counseling in Cambridge, Mass., the best advice I received was just three words long. I was told to always have "constant forward motion." This means to execute, even when the results won't be perfect. When it comes to clinical care, you need to be superb — but everything else can and will be improved upon later.

For example:

- You have an ugly logo? GREAT! An ugly logo is better than no logo.
- Your business cards say Vista Print on them? GREAT! Crappy free Vista Print business cards are better than no business cards.
- You were misquoted in XYZ publication? GREAT! You can now say you've been mentioned in XYZ. How fancy!

I sometimes speak with counselors stuck on a tough Catch-22 such as, "I can't get an office until I find some clients, but I can't recruit clients without an office to see them." Yes, you can. In fact, you have to! Either decision will work, but doing neither means you'll never move forward.

The bootstrapper knows when to stop writing the business plan and when to start building the business.

5) Reject excuses

"There are more counselors per capita in my town than anywhere in the USA." This is my favorite excuse of all time because I hear it every week from therapists all across the country. (By the way, if anyone knows what city actually has the most therapists, please e-mail me at Anthony@thriveworks.com.)

My second favorite excuse is, "Building a caseload is impossible in this economy!" What does the economy have to do with anything? Maybe a small percentage of people have lost their health insurance, but most haven't. Also, rent is cheaper, as is advertising, and people need someone to talk to about the economy!

Other excuses: I'm too old. I'm only 30, and I look young (i.e., I'm too young). I don't have capital. All the good insurance panels are closed. Managed care has ruined the profession. Life coaches are stealing my business. Corporations aren't referring like they used to. Rent is too expensive. I have too much debt. I have a family to provide for. And the list goes on!

Each of these is a challenge. However, bootstrappers don't succeed because their path is easy. They succeed because they refuse to let excuses overtake them.

6) Build risk tolerance

Allow me to stereotype. Counselors hate risk. For a bootstrapper, items at risk are time, effort, pride and, to a lesser extent, money. The startup costs for a counseling practice can be as low as a few thousand dollars to rent an office, do some advertising and delegate a few of the more heinous tasks such as medical credentialing and billing.

Here's the full truth: There's no risk concerning whether you will fail. You will. That's part of the process! Thomas J. Watson, the founder of IBM, once said, "If you want to succeed, double your failure rate."

Bootstrappers know that if they work hard, and smart, in the end, they are likely to succeed. Starting a private practice might be risky, but (in this economy!) it's no riskier than being an employee.

7) Avoid nonessential partners

The only ship that doesn't sail is a partnership! When consulting with someone starting a practice, often at some point he or she will say, "Thanks! I'm going to share this with my business partners."

It's often believed that partners help to spread out the risk of starting a practice. They don't. In some ways, they increase the risk. Having partners can dilute one's sense of responsibility and are sometimes used to avoid necessary hard work (partners are also useful for sharing the blame when, after two years, the practice still isn't thriving).

Partners are not necessarily bad, but they often exist for the wrong reasons. Bootstrappers ask themselves why they need a partner. Is it because they're scared or lack confidence? Is it because they don't want to be responsible for their business (if so, maybe they should remain employees after all)? No, bootstrappers get a partner only when someone brings a huge amount of value to the table and is willing to work as hard as the bootstrapper is to skyrocket the company.

Note: Two counselors often make a poor partner match because they have the same strengths. (Even if one works with kids and the other knows eye movement desensitization and reprocessing, they're still both clinicians.) Instead, how about a counselor and a medical biller? Or an accountant? Or an experienced manager? Or someone great at starting small businesses?

8) Track your progress

Milestones are achievable company advancements. For the nascent counseling practice, they may include signing an office lease, furnishing an office, getting on 10 insurance panels, publishing an ad in a local magazine and so on.

Action steps are all the smaller efforts required to reach a milestone. For example, publishing an ad in a local magazine involves

1. Selecting the publication
2. Contacting the publication
3. Determining a fair price
4. Negotiating a price
5. Writing the ad

6. Hiring someone to design the ad
7. Submitting the ad for publication
8. Paying the bill.

Write out your 10 most important milestones as well as the action steps necessary to complete them. Then, assign a deadline to each one. Include how many hours of bootstrapping each milestone will take to complete. This is your guide to help you stay on track and also to affirm your progress on days when it feels like you're spinning your wheels and getting nowhere.

Complete a few milestones and you'll be well on your way. You're a bona fide bootstrapper, starting your private practice!

Lesson 4:
How to Measure and Cope with Risk as an Entrepreneur

Writing this, I am sitting at a coffee kiosk at the Reading Terminal Market in Philadelphia, PA. I'm here because this week Thriveworks is opening a new company-owned location, right here in Philly. As a small company, any endeavor that includes the words "new location" is a serious risk.

I don't like risk, and the risks of opening a new practice are many. We need the right location, the right staff, the right operations, the right credentialing, and even the right marketing. The failure of any one of these key areas will cripple the project. While risk abounds, I try not to fear it, and over the years I've improved (perhaps only slightly) in my ability to access and manage risk. In this lesson, I'll write what I know about risk as it relates to business in the counseling profession.

1) Being an Employee is Risky Too

Some claim that being an employee is just as risky as starting a business. I disagree. Nevertheless, there are risks of employment. An employee can end up on the wrong side of office politics and get passed over for advancement, or lose one's job entirely. In the health professions, it's not uncommon for organizations to change directions based on funding. A mental health clinic once catering to college students might transition into treatment for the homeless. In this scenario, one gets to keep his or her job, but the work that was once loved is replaced with an entirely different set of duties and expectations. As one counselor said to me, "I'm still employed, but I'm making less money and spending half my time on case management I never wanted to do."

Still, employees can't lose money. Startup costs are zero (to the employee, the employer has several costs), and if things don't work out an employee can simply walk away and find another place to work. If you're looking to minimize risk, don't start a practice. Instead, re-read the lesson, *"Should I start a Private Practice?"* which provides 9 tips for becoming a highly paid agency employee.

2) Failure is Part of Success...but Doesn't Guarantee It

Thomas Edison, in an over-quoted anecdote, was once asked about his many failed attempts at inventing the light bulb. He replied "I didn't fail, I found 2000 ways how not to make a light bulb." He is also credited with saying "Many of life's failures are people who did not realize how close they were to success when they gave up."

Is it really darkest before the dawn? Ask Frank Nelson Cole. In 1903, Cole gave a presentation at an American Mathematical Society conference where he proved that a very famous prime number, $2^{67}-1$, was not actually prime. During Cole's "lecture," he approached the chalkboard and (in complete silence) wrote out longhand the number $2^{67}-1$, which is 147,573,952,589,676,412,927. Cole then moved to the other side of the board and wrote 193,707,721 × 761,838,257,287. He multiplied the numbers by hand, showing that the result equaled $2^{67}-1$! The attendees erupted with applause. Cole later said that finding the factors of $2^{67}-1$ had taken him "three years of Sundays."

While the stories of Edison and Cole show the value of persistence, not all persistence is bears fruit. According to Seth Godin, entrepreneurs need to tell the difference between a "dip" and a "cul-de-sac." If you're in a dip, you can push yourself out. If you're in a cul-de-sac, it doesn't matter how much you push. Godin states that being told to never quit is "Bad advice. Winners quit all the time. *They just quit the right stuff at the right time.*" As you begin (or grow) your practice, some areas of your business might be cul-de-sacs: specific target populations, groups, psycho-educational programs, online services, specific marketing endeavors, specific counseling methods, etc. Learning to differentiate cul-de-sacs from dips will help you to focus on the areas of your business that can grow, and jettison areas that are wasting your time and effort.

3) Betting the Ranch Versus Taking a Punt

Betting the Ranch: *The act of wagering a large portion of your assets. Failure places you into serious financial trouble.*

Taking a Punt: *The act of wagering a small portion of your assets. Failure doesn't place you into serious financial trouble.*

There is a big difference between betting the ranch, and taking a punt. On one end, if you bet the ranch enough times, you will eventually lose the ranch. On the other end, if you're so cautious that you never take a punt, you'll never get anywhere.

Counselors are more often on the cautious end of the spectrum. I've known many to be too conservative to take a $400 punt that could build their practice (this could be for a better office, a website, a print ad, a booth at a conference, etc.). While for some clinicians $400 is betting the ranch, for many it's a manageable risk.

How much can you afford to take a punt with? $40? $400? $4000? The amount of cash you have on hand is not nearly as important as how you interact with the money you have. Ask yourself, "How is my risk tolerance? Am I betting the ranch? Am I afraid to take a punt?"

4) Risk Versus Reward

Would you buy a car for $10,000, with the potential to resell it for $10,250? No! What if the clutch goes out? Or you overestimated the car's value? The reward is too small relative to the risk. However, would you buy a car for $250, if it has a blue book value of $10,000? Of course! Even if the car doesn't run, you can sell it for parts, or scrap. The potential reward heavily outweighs the risk. So what are the risks and rewards of starting a counseling practice? Service businesses, such as counseling, tend to have low startup costs. There's no manufacturing, no patents, no inventory. However, counselors today struggle to build caseloads, and they struggle to get paid for services rendered.

Therefore, in some aspects starting a counseling practice is low risk, and in others it's high risk. If you're considering starting a private practice, invest time before you invest your money. Learn the costs of doing business in your area, and learn the potential rewards (consider the lesson "Building a Six Figure Private Practice" which itemizes some of the costs). Finally, while risk abounds, try not to fear it. Take a punt. In time you'll improve in your ability to access and manage risk.

Lesson 5:
How Much Money Can I Earn in Private Practice?

According to Salary.com, a Licensed Professional Counselor working in Cambridge, MA makes a median average of $40,798 per year. In a city where rent for a small apartment runs north of 2K a month, that's beyond bleak.

While nobody chooses counseling as a profession because of the high pay, is dismal compensation our fate? Financially speaking, are counselors better off giving advice while tending bar? I don't think so.

With good planning and hard work, earning over $100,000 profit in year two of private practice is for many an obtainable goal.

Money in Private Practice

As counselors, we loathe to discuss money–we want to focus on patient care. However, it's a necessary part of keeping the doors open. Truth is, you can't help anyone if you're out of business, and a counseling practice is precisely that—a business. Hence, we're going to look at the financial aspects of running a viable business/practice.

Note: the following numbers are only estimates for a solo-practitioner in private practice. You might need to adjust expenses, client fees, and volumes based on your own goals and the costs of your area. I've tried to be conservative when referencing revenues, and liberal when referencing expenses.

Client Fees

Don't go it alone: Open your own Thriveworks Counseling Practice! Client fees vary depending on location and payer. For example, in Virginia a masters-level clinician accepting 3rd party insurance payments might earn $99 for a diagnostic evaluation (90791). Ongoing appointments for individual or family psychotherapy (90834/90837/90847) might pay around $70. Let's estimate your average session fee to be a moderate $75 per session.

Fulltime Caseload

The number of sessions that constitutes a fulltime caseload is often debated amongst clinicians. Some persons feel that 30 sessions per week is a heavy caseload, while others find that they can serve 40+ clients per week. I find 35 clients per week to be a reasonable number. If you're providing 45-minute sessions, that's 26.25 hours of face-to-face work with clients each week. Add in schedule gaps and practice management duties, and you're looking at a 40 to 45-hour workweek. It's a full time job, but sustainable.

In addition, let's say that you give yourself a modest 4 weeks of vacation every year.

Simple Math:

35 (sessions per week) x 48 (weeks per year) = 1,680 (sessions per year)

* * *

1,680 (sessions per year) x $75 (fee per session) = $126,000 (gross yearly revenue)

Normal Practice Expenses

Office and Operational Expenses

There are numerous small and seemingly hidden costs to running a private practice: from patient parking, to coffee, to organic tissues, to printer ink. Here are some ballpark numbers for the solo private practice.

- Rent (one office): $550 per month = $6,600 per year
- Office supplies (computer, software, phone, furniture, printer, coffee, etc.) = $3,000 per year Note: furniture, unless financed, will be an initial outlay of several thousand dollars.
- Professional dues, continuing education, & liability insurance = $800 per year
- ($800 won't get you to a national conference, but it will cover the basics. There are many options for low cost CEs–one just needs to look).
- Accounting & Legal fees = $500 per year
- Other Miscellaneous = $1000 per year

Total Office and Operational Expenses: $11,900 per year

In addition, two potentially larger expense categories are in the realm of marketing and billing.

Advertising and Marketing

Looking for a Turn-Key Counseling Practice? Thriveworks is Franchising!

There's no "correct" amount to spend on marketing and advertising. In fact, many counselors get by with spending very little. However, for the sake of this exercise, let's say that you'll take 5 percent of your gross yearly revenue and invest it into marketing and advertising your practice.

Simple Math:

5 percent (marketing and advertising) of $126,000 (yearly revenue) = $6,300 (marketing per year).

Medical Billing

While some counselors prefer to do their own medical billing, you may wish to hire a company to handle it for you. A customary cost is 8 percent of what the billing company collects, which comes out to around 5.5 percent of your gross revenue (note that it's 5.5 percent because medical billing companies don't customarily take a share of client deductibles, or co-pays).

Simple Math:

5.5 percent (billing company) of $126,000 (yearly revenue) = $6,930 (billing company fee)

Simple Totals:

$126,000 (gross revenue)-$11,900 (office & ops expenses) –$6,300 (marketing per year) –$6,930 (billing company fee)

= $100,870 (final net revenue)

And there we have it: a 6-figure private practice. A far cry from $40,798!

Variables

While the above provides an outline of private practice financials, no counseling practice will perfectly mirror the example. To help you determine more accurately your practice's finances, here is a list of financial variables for your consideration:

1. The "final net revenue" above does not include the cost of health insurance, retirement planning, accounting services, or taxes, which are often partially covered by an employer. These items will detract from your expendable income.

2. Owning a business might have tax advantages that one doesn't receive as an employee. For example, if you purchase a new laptop it might qualify as a business expense (meaning it's paid for with pre-tax money).

3. The estimates above assume that one will be able to maintain a client roster of 35 client sessions a week (by year two). Low new client volume, or high client attrition, can reduce your weekly session count.

4. Client cancellations and/or client no-shows could lower (or raise) your income, depending on how you manage your practice schedule.

5. To expedite the building of a caseload in year one, more money could be invested into advertising (or time spent in professional networking).

6. After building a strong reputation and establishing active referral sources, you may be able to eliminate advertising and marketing (reclaim up to 5 percent).

7. If you see some (or all) cash-pay clients, you can reduce or eliminate medical billing expenses (reclaim up to 5.5 percent).

8. If demand for your services outweighs supply (that's you), you can raise your cash-pay rates to $99 (add $40,320 revenue!). Note: you can also add a second clinician, but that starts a whole new level of mathematical complexity.

9. The estimates above do not account for unpaid session fees (subtract up to 4 percent).

10. If you accept credit cards, subtract roughly 2 percent revenue from whatever percentage of session fees you expect to process with plastic.

11. If you decide to work 40, 45-minute sessions per week (30 face-to-face hours with clients), add $18,000 revenue.

12. If you reduce your time off from 4 weeks to 3 weeks, add $2,625 revenue (not worth it!).

Lesson 6:
Picking a Name for Your Practice

Naming your practice is like getting a tattoo. It's painful. And, excluding expensive surgery, it's something you're stuck with for life. In this month's column, I'll provide some pointers on picking a good name for your practice.

1) You don't need a name to open shop

Finding the right name is a process. Resist the temptation to rush into a name that you might later regret. When trying to find a name for my practice, I spent a couple months writing possibilities on napkins and in the margins of books I was reading. There were long nights tossing back and forth ideas with friends and confidants. All the while my practice was open, just unnamed (like so many counseling practices, people just referred to it as "Anthony Centore's office"). Eventually, I came upon what I thought would be the perfect name: "Thrive Counseling."

2) Make sure your name isn't taken

Before deciding on a name, you'll want to check if the name (or a confusingly similar one) is already in use by another practice in your area. Moreover, it's wise to check whether someone else has already registered your potential name with the US Patent and Trademark Office. To do this, you can hire a firm (for around $500) to do an "exhaustive search" or just do your own "basic search" for free at USPTO.gov.

A word of caution: If you choose a name that infringes on someone else's trademark you're likely to get a "cease and desist" letter from their attorney. On that note, once you choose a name for your practice, consider protecting it by applying for a trademark yourself. This will cost you some money, but the cost is nominal compared to the expense of rebranding your practice later.

When I first named my practice I didn't check USPTO.gov, only to later learn that a small California-based company known as Keiser Permanente had already registered "Thrive" under the broad category "healthcare services"! Where did this leave me? You guessed it, back to scrawling on napkins. If I wanted my brand to have any legal protection, I needed to change my name!

3) Get the .com

Things change, but for the last 15 years the ".com" has been the domain suffix of choice. Today, and likely for a while, having a .com website that correlates with your brand name is highly desirable. For example, if you're considering the name "Aspire," for your practice, you'll want to acquire "aspire.com." Of course, unless you want to pay a couple hundred grand, you'll never get a domain name like "aspire.com." That's okay! You can register "aspirecounseling.com," "aspiretherapy.com," or settle for a variant like "goaspire.com." If you can't seem to find anything simple that matches your potential name, you may want to choose a different practice name—it's that important.

When I chose the name "Thriveworks," Thriveworks.com was already registered by a graphic design firm in California. I paid the firm several thousand dollars for the domain name and it was well worth having a .com that matched my brand.

4) Choose a name that will work long term

I run across too many "Bayside Counseling Centers" that are no longer near a bay, "Amherst Counseling Centers" with a second location outside Amherst, and practices called "ThePlayTherapyGroup" that at some point expanded to serve children and adults. Before choosing a name, ask yourself, "Is this name likely to work if I change locations, or if my company evolves?"

5) Avoid trends

The name Lamps-a-Rama probably sounded really hip when it came out, as did every computer store name with the prefix "micro-" or "digi-." But today, they all just sound dated. Avoid fashion!

6) Avoid your personal name

This is a matter of opinion, but I find that "Smith Counseling," or "Smith and Associates," can hold a practice back. Name your practice after yourself and you'll face an uphill battle to convince new potential clients that any counselors working for you aren't second fiddle.

7) Your name should be poetry

A great brand name looks good from all angles. When RIM (Research in Motion) was searching for a name for their most popular handheld communication device, they hired the California-based firm Lexicon Branding to help. The team steered away from names related to the word "e-mail," since research showed that the word could increase customers' blood pressure. Instead, the team searched for something "more joyful that might decrease blood pressure." When someone pointed out that the buttons on RIM's device looked like seeds, they began exploring fruity names:

strawberry, melon, etc. They finally landed on "Blackberry."

Says David Placek, of Lexicon, "BlackBerry sticks better than something like ProMail or MegaMail." Blackberry is a great name. It's enjoyable, and "black" as a color is often associated with premium quality. The one limitation with "Blackberry" is that object is isn't immediately obvious by the name.

One of my favorite brand names is "Zappos." Originally "shoesite.com," CEO Tony Hsieh knew the name was too limited, and changed it to "Zappos" early in the company's life. The name Zappos relates subtly to their primary focus on shoes (as a derivative of the Spanish word "zapatos") without limiting the brand to the footwear category. Also, the "Zap" in the name communicates speed and performance. Need something? Zap! Here it is!

8) A Name isn't everything

When you start a practice, you're striving to create a brand that can be bigger than you, and that might even outlive you. A good name can help. That said, a name isn't everything. It's a small piece of the much larger puzzle of building a great company. There's no shortage of examples of companies that have less than great names, but that are still great companies.

Lesson 7:
Six Nasty Rumors About Accepting Clients' Health Insurance

From recent graduates to seasoned clinicians, today it seems that everyone in part-or full-time private practice is asking the same question: "Should I accept health insurance?" It's a complicated question. The decision whether to accept third party payments will have a big impact on your counseling practice. The question is made even more difficult as there isn't just a lot of information to consider—there is also a lot of misinformation about working with insurance companies.

Below are a few semi-misguided statements I've heard from counselors worried about accepting insurance. I've tried to provide a helpful response to each statement:

1) "I've heard I should stay away from accepting insurance."
In the same way that your parents might have told you "don't do drugs," some counselor's mentors have warned them "don't do insurance." The idea of starting a cash-only practice is enticing! There's less fuss with billing, and you can set your own prices for services. The downside is that building a private practice, even with insurance, is hard work—starting a "cash-only" private practice can be even harder. While some clinicians succeed, many counselors struggle to maintain a large enough cash-paying client base to make a living. This may be okay if a counselor wants only a part-time practice, or has a separate source of income.

2) "I've heard that insurance companies don't pay well."

There are a few companies that pay particularly poorly. However, the idea that insurance companies don't pay well might be overstated. In Boston, the average intake appointment (90801) pays about $100 for a clinician with a Master's degree. Ongoing appointments for individual therapy (90806) pay around $75-87, and appointments for couples counseling (i.e., "family therapy with patient present", 90847) pay about $10 more. Note: these are 45-minute sessions, not 1-hour sessions. If a counselor can fill their client roster with clients who are willing to pay these rates (or higher) in cash, great! For them, accepting insurance probably doesn't make sense. On the other hand, insurance might be a good option if there are gaps in one's schedule, or if one's sliding scale keeps dipping significantly lower than what insurance would otherwise pay.

3) "I've heard that insurance companies are impossible to deal with."

Not exactly. When it's business as usual, insurance companies are easy to deal with (you submit claims, and receive payment). However, at times when there is confusion over an unpaid claim, insurance can be a hassle. Calling may amount to some hold time, and perhaps a few frustrating exchanges with the "provider relations department." Still, working with insurance is not impossible. If you don't want to interact with them personally, you could consider hiring a billing company. The cost is usually about 8% of what they collect. Since this doesn't include client co-pays and deductibles (cash you'll receive from clients), it ends up somewhere around 6% of your gross revenue.

4) "I don't want to be a 'slave to'/'employee of' insurance companies."

Being networked with insurance companies, you are neither a slave, nor an employee. You are simply affiliated (i.e., credentialed), which means that you have been given approval to bill insurance for authorized services that you render to their insured customers. Where some providers find frustration is that insurance companies are not willing to authorize care to patients with certain diagnoses, such as "V codes" (e.g., relationship problem, academic problem, etc.). Hence, to receive payment for services, some counselors find themselves trying to justify a biological diagnosis, such as Major Depressive Disorder, even if the patient's presenting symptoms fall short of the diagnostic criteria.

5) "I don't want to do all the additional documentation."

Don't confuse a private practice that accepts insurance, with a more bureaucratic setting such as a hospital, or a government-run medical clinic. As a licensed counselor, you are already taking clinical notes—at least a diagnostic evaluation, treatment plan, and SOAP notes each session (right?). That's all you need. In fact, insurance companies aren't generally going to ask to see this, and they can't dictate to you how you should do your record keeping. What insurance companies will ask for are dates of service, patient diagnoses, and procedure codes.

6) "I don't want to be told what clients I have to see."

This is a common misconception. Even if you are networked with an insurance company, you are never required to see any particular patient or client. You still get to decide what clients you want to see, and what clients you would rather refer.

Dispelling Rumors about Insurance, Not Advocating for It.

In the above paragraphs, we reviewed 6 common rumors about accepting insurance. However, I'm not advocating that insurance is the right fit for you and your practice. Such a decision requires a much longer consideration, outside the scope of this lesson!

Lesson 8:
Three Real Challenges with Accepting Clients' Health Insurance

Busy counseling practices today, with some exceptions, are insurance driven. There are good things that come from working with insurance companies. Clients who might not have been able to afford your services now have access. Also, it's much easier to induce clients to buy services when someone else is paying the bill.

However, it's not all perfect. There's operational costs to checking benefits, submitting claims, chasing AR (accounts receivable), and responding to audits. While these are costly hassles, these aren't the real challenges that come with building an insurance-based practice. In this month's column, I'll address a 3 of the "real" challenges and provide a few (partial) solutions.

1. Your Business Has 5 Customers

In most areas, the top 5 payers will account for 80% of your business. Having the majority of your practice supported by a few large payers means that if the relationship with any one of them goes south—say a payer lowers reimbursement rates, brings mental health services in-house, or otherwise terminates their relationship with you, you've lost a large chunk of your revenue.

Large customers lower the financial value of your business: John Warrillow, author of the book *Built to Sell,* calls it "The downside of dependence." If your company manufactures tubing, and Toyota's purchases account for 50% of your sales, your company's worth less than if no customer constituted more than 10%.

"But wait," You might ask, "aren't your clients your customers?" Sort of. If you own a toy store and a child picks out a toy and mom buys it, who's your customer? The child gets the toy, but mom's making the purchase. With insurance-based mental health, clients have not bought into the idea that they're your customers. Clients are disconnected from what your services really cost—they don't know what you're reimbursed, nor do they feel responsible for charges if insurance fails to pay (despite what your informed consent says). This bring us to the second real problem…

2) You Have No Negotiation Power

In major sectors of the US healthcare industry (in most states), hospital systems, pharmaceutical companies, and insurance companies battle over prices. If a hospital system is big enough in a given area, it can demand higher rates. If a pharmaceutical company has medications without generic alternatives, they too can raise prices. If an insurance company covers the majority of the lives in a market, they can demand lower prices. In general, the three need each other, and all three have power to negotiate.

Outpatient mental health is different. We're in a fragmented industry with lots of supply (i.e., lots of counselors working alone or in small practices). Mental health providers often have zero negotiating power. When we do "negotiate" with insurance companies, the conversation isn't *"this is the rate you need to pay me to join your network"* it's *"will you please let me in your network?"* If you drop out of a network because the company is a pain-in-the-neck to get reimbursed from or because the rates are too low, somehow there's 10 other counselors in private practice scrambling to take your place. This leads us to the next problem…

3. You Don't Control Your Price

Legend has it, long ago a therapist would accept a client's insurance and then charge the client the remaining balance of the his/her full rate. Such a practice (balance billing) is long since forbidden for providers in network with insurance companies.

As a business owner, having prices that you can't control should make you uneasy. In a free market, prices vary. A coat from *Burlington Coat Factory* doesn't cost the same as one from *Nordstrom*. Brand quality, customer service, and the overall experience of the two stores differs.

If prices are fixed, you might feel okay if you're running a business on the lower end. If you're *Nordstrom*, however, you're finding it problematic to build and operate a high-quality *Nordstrom* store at a fixed (presumably lower) price. Fixed pricing leads to lower standards.

Other fragmented healthcare industries don't experience the same price controls as mental health counseling.

- Massage therapists and acupuncturists still don't take insurance in most cases.
- When patients visit their dentists they're told that insurance "will help" with the cost but benefits get maxed out quickly (meaning clients are used to paying out of pocket).

- The chiropractor's unit of service is so brief (~10 minutes), one's $20 copay represents a large portion of their fee, which means insurance reimbursements are a small slice of their revenue (The chain *The Joint* doesn't even accept insurance anymore and the out-of-pocket difference to clients isn't cost prohibitive).

- Lastly, for optometrists, many insurance plans don't cover every service (like contact lens exams), and almost never does insurance cover the full cost of glasses and contacts.

Is the answer to reclaim control of your price and run a cash practice? That's difficult. In counseling, if a client has a $20 copay and your cash rate is $100 per session, you're asking the client to pay a 500% increase in out-of-pocket expense. Understandably, the pool of clients willing to tolerate this increase is small.

What's the solution?

Is there one solution? No, but here are some partial solutions that might help you build a business in a decidedly insurance-based mental health industry. Admittedly, none are great.

1. If someone's paying you to be *Burlington Coat Factory* (or *Goodwill*), don't give them *Nordstrom*: rent cheaper space, provide less customer service. In general, adjust your service in accordance with the amount you're being paid.

2. Find a way to upsell your clients on something insurance won't pay for. This will need to be optional, so you'll have to offer something that clients really want.

3. Leave the mental health field entirely. Do something where you can help people and also earn compensation in alignment with your education, training, and effort.

4. Continue to offer counseling, but diversify your practice with services for which you can control the terms such as public speaking, consulting, crisis intervention, or executive / leadership coaching.

5. Try taking out-of-network benefits only. It's an uphill path as a decreasing number of clients have them, and such benefits—when one has them—are often limited.

6. Only work with insurance payers that reimburse an amount with which you're satisfied. You'll make more revenue per session, but it might lower the market value of your business (see problem 1).

Lesson 9:
A Case for Accepting Clients' Health Insurance

Even when taking into consideration the warnings in the previous lesson *"Three Real Challenges with Accepting Clients' Health Insurance,"* whether you're a therapist in private practice, or working for a company, there are many reasons that getting on insurance panels is important to your success.

1) Getting on Panels Gives you Leverage

Sometimes mental health counselors who work for hospitals or large therapy practices think that getting on insurance panels isn't important, or that they are already listed with insurance companies--this isn't true! If you are working for a large practice or company, you are likely working under their contract with insurance companies. Therefore, you ***personally*** are not paneled. This means that if you were to leave your job, you would find yourself unable to accept new clients' insurance, even if you've been billing insurance for years.

Being independently credentialed means that you are protected if you ever decide to leave your current job, and even means that you have some leverage (a "bargaining chip") with your employer when you discuss compensation increases.

2) HMOs Greatly Outnumber PPOs

Persons with PPO (Preferred Provider Organization) plans can see counselors, psychologist, and psychiatrists that are no part of their network (that is, un-credentialed licensed professionals), under some circumstances, and usually for additional cost to the patient / client.

However, the PPO plans have quickly become a plan of the past as HMO (Health Maintenance Organization) plans have increased in popularity. Moreover, persons with PPO plans now face significant penalties and fees for choosing a provider out-of-network, such as higher deductibles and only a fractional split of mental health care fees. The bottom line--if clients are going to use their insurance, they will want (if not need) you to be in network and paneled with their insurance company.

3) Universal Healthcare and Mental Health Parity means that everyone can see a Therapist

Two huge changes in healthcare make it crucial for all mental health counselors / therapists to be credentialed on at least some insurance plans. The first is the universal healthcare bill, which will make it so that persons in the USA--universally--will have health care coverage (and will want to use it!). The second change is the Mental Health Parity laws, which states that mental health care is not an optional part of health care, but is obligatorily covered with other major medical coverage. If you are unable to accept insurance, it is going to be a hard sell to acquire clients with this coverage.

4) Panels Will Close

Saying "get on panels now or else" sounds dramatic, but the truth is that many panels are already closing, or closed. In Boston, many of the major players: Harvard-Pilgrim, United Behavioral Health, BCBS HMO, and Tufts are not accepting new providers. What this means is that for new counselors entering the field, they are literally unable to see any clients from those huge pools of clients. And it means that the counselors on the panels have few problems filling their schedules.

You might wonder "Why would insurance companies limit the number of providers on their panels?" That's a good question--the companies often state that paneling mental health professionals' costs them money administratively, and once they have enough providers they would be wasting money if they brought on more. However, others say that the more the insurance companies limit the number of providers who are on their panels, the less likely a patient will be able to use their insurance benefits. Whatever the reason, the ugly truth is that if you want to be on insurance panels, you're wise to start sooner, not later.

Five Reasons Medical Credentialing Software is Useless for Most Practices

Medical credentialing (the process of getting on insurance panels) is a hassle for many health providers. In response to this, several credentialing software companies have popped-up over the last few years, promising that their software will make the credentialing process easier. But will it?

In this lesson, we will look at how medical credentialing software works, and review several reasons why—unless your company has over 100 health providers—credentialing software won't save you time, or make the credentialing process easier.

Full disclosure: I own of several counseling practices. I began looking into medical credentialing software several years ago, and have spoken with several of the major companies as late as a summer 2012. In addition, and possibly most relevant for the student concerned about author bias, I also run a company that provides medical credentialing services to health professionals (at http://medicalcredentialing.org). After much investigation, even though we have credentialed thousands of healthcare professionals, we have determined that credentialing software cannot make our service more efficient for our employees, or our customers.

Now, let's look at why medical credentialing software is a time waster, not a time saver.

1) Medical Credentialing Software Requires Hours-to-Days of Training
In general, the way credentialing software works is as follows: Paper-based provider enrollment applications are scanned into the software system, and "Mapped." Mapping, in essence, means to take a paper-based application and turn it into an electronic form, where provider information can be typed (or imported) onto the application.

While the concept is straight forward, the execution is complicated. Training on how to use the software is laborious. One of the largest medical credentialing companies requests that new customers send their administrative staff for a weekend-long training course. Hence, learning to use the software takes more time than most health practices will ever spend filling out provider applications manually. This, already, makes medical credentialing software unhelpful. However, in addition...

2) Using The Software Doesn't Save Time

Even after someone is trained on how to use credentialing software, using the software still will not save time for practices with under 100 providers. If a medical practice has 100 providers or more, and each needs to be added to a specific group (let's say 10) of insurance panels, medical credentialing software could save some time. Instead of needing to fill out 10 applications for each provider (one for each insurance company), one application can be completed for each provider, and that information imported electronically onto the other 9 applications, thereby saving transcription time.

The problem for the practice with less than 100 providers is that mapping a single new insurance application into the system can take several hours, and even then it might not work 100% correctly—and will need additional tweaking. Because of this, all the timesaving benefits are spent setting up the software. This brings us to the next problem…

3) The Software Programs don't have all the Applications you Need

Medical Credentialing Software companies claim that they have hundreds or thousands of provider applications in their systems, representing insurance companies across the USA. This may be true, but even the largest medical credentialing companies—when you really get down to brass tasks with them—admit they usually have less than half of the forms that any given customer needs (if you are working in behavioral health, for instance, forget about it. There is a dearth of behavioral health applications in these systems).

Even if the software appears to have the application you require, beware! Health insurance companies are often updating their provider application forms—sometimes as frequently as every 6 months—and credentialing software has no feature for tracking or keeping up with this. Hence, submit an application generated from medical credentialing software and you might find that the application is rejected because it isn't the most up-to-date form. In addition...

4) Medical Credentialing Software is Useless for Online Applications

Many insurance companies are switching from paper-based documents to (exclusively) online provider application forms. This renders medical credentialing software useless, as there are no paper applications to map. And finally...

5) Completing the Provider Application is Just the Beginning.

Medical credentialing software companies claim that they save health organizations time by helping those organizations get health providers' information down on paper faster.

While, for the reasons stated above, I don't think this is true for any practice under 100 providers, even for larger organizations the reasons medical credentialing is time-consuming have little to do with filling out provider applications.

Instead... The Essence of Medical Credentialing

Getting on insurance panels is a grueling process because

1. Convincing insurance companies to accept your application can be a challenge, as many good panels are stating that they are 'closed'

2. Provider applications are always changing, and every application is different

3. Credentialing requires a plethora of accompanying documentation, which needs to be provided exactly as requested

4. Credentialing applications are often lost by insurance companies, or get stuck in the review proves

5. Successfully getting on insurance panels requires frequent calls to insurance companies to check-up on applications, and to help push the applications through to completion.

When it comes to these tasks, medical credentialing software is dead in the water.

Lesson 10:
10 Tips for Your Counseling Practice Website

Giving website tips is tricky. While some counselors are overwhelmed by the thought of managing a website, others are quite savvy. Still, I wanted to share some thoughts because, in general, counseling websites tend to be a little soft when compared to other small business industries like private practice attorneys, yoga studios, and realtors—to name a few. As a group, we have some catching up to do.

In this month's column, I'm speaking to two groups of counselors, giving basic first steps to web novices (see "beginner tips"), and a few tricks to more web savvy counselors (see "pro tips"). I hope you enjoy.

1) Design

Beginner Tip: Have a Website

SquareSpace, WordPress, and Sites.Google.com are just three of the multitude of platforms on which one can build a DIY website. These platforms require zero knowledge of "coding" and are extremely affordable at just a few dollars a month.

Don't think you need a website? Consider this: Even if a client hears about you through word of mouth, clients today are likely to look you up online before scheduling an appointment. These days, not having a website is a bad first impression.

Pro Tip: Update Your Site Design Every 12 Months

Like clothing, web designs go in and out of fashion. Remember when all websites had vertical navigation on the left side of the page? Today horizontal navigation dominates. Remember when web pages where skinny and long? Today pages are much wider, or set to the entire browser width. One website feature that is "out of fashion" in 2014 is the slider (rotating pictures) that many websites have covering the top of their homepages. Death to sliders! In the same way you don't want to be caught wearing jeans with holes, or an Ed Hardy t-shirt, in 2014, you might want to find something other than a slider for the top of your homepage. So, while you don't need to redesign your site from scratch, invest in a design update once a year.

2) Content

Beginner Tip: Deliver Useful Content

Your website should be more than an online business card. Include useful articles that speak to your target audience. Or get crazy and post a video: If your computer is less than 5 years old you likely have all the technology you need. Best practice is to get on a schedule. Create a new piece of content once a week, once a month, or even once a quarter. Just make sure you have a plan to grow your website and make it more valuable to visitor's overtime.

Pro Tip: Check Headings and Titles for Typos

Headings are the first place users find typos. Ironically, they seem to be the last place that writers check for them! I have read too many beautifully written articles, with a typo in the title! In fact, I've been guilty of this. One time I accidentally titled a webpage "Meet the Counselors." My team caught this and asked, "Hey, is that a Freudian slip!?" Don't be like me—proofread those headings and titles!

3) Location

Beginner Tip: Address and Phone Number on Each Page

Don't make visitors to your website hunt around to find your practice's address or phone number. Make sure the information is visible on every page—the footer is a common location that works well. A phone number in the header (top) of each page is also a convenient location.

Pro Tip: Include Pictures and a Map to the Office

Having an image of the outside of your building can help clients find your office when arriving for a first session. Also, interior pictures, if they are well done, will show clients the care you've spent outfitting a clean, comfortable space. Lastly, a research study comparing the effectiveness of 2 brochures encouraging college students to get a tetanus shot found that including a map to the university medical center in the brochure increased student compliance. The map was highly effective even though all the students already knew where the medical center was located!

4) Navigation / Links

Beginner Tip: Create an "Our Counselors" or "About Me" Page

The "Our Counselors" or, in the case of a solo-practice, the "About Me" page is often one of the highest trafficked pages on a counseling website. Clients are attracted to these pages as they typically include headshots and bios of the practice's clinicians. Make sure this page is easy to find, and accessible from every other page on the website. In addition, see my CT column on Counselors' Top 10 Marketing Mistakes for tips on bios and headshots.

Pro Tip: Remove that "Verified by X Directory" Badge

Counseling directories often ask subscribers to post a 'badge' on their websites that links back to the directory. These typically read something like "Verified by Psychology Today." These badges add no value to you. On the contrary, it can lead visitors off your website to view the profiles of other counselors in your area! If you want to build credibility, post a list of publications you've been quoted in, note that you're an ACA Member, or post a link for users to verify that your state licensure is in good standing.

5) Personalization

Beginner Tip: Have fun with it!

Developing a website for your practice doesn't need to be scary, or laborious. Once you get going, posting your thoughts and resources for clients could become an enjoyable and rewarding part of running your practice!

Pro Tip: Temper Personal Tastes

Things I have seen: Counselor websites where his or her dog or cat is the practice's mascot, counselor websites with a heavy equine (horse) theme, and my personal favorite—a counseling website completely based on the instincts and personality of the wolf (yes, a wolf theme). These animals / themes might speak to you, but they're not likely to appeal to the majority of people looking for, say, couples counseling.

Scratching the Surface

What have you found to be most helpful in building a web presence? What have been your biggest challenges? Email me your thoughts, ideas, or questions—they could become the basis for a future column.

Lesson 11:
Sprint! Opening a Counseling Practice in 7 Days

Zero to One Client in Seven Days

I was speaking with a licensed counselor and she asked me "If I wanted to get started in private practice, how long would it take me to open my doors and see my first client?" I thought about the question for a minute, and replied "With a couple thousand dollars and a close to full-time commitment, you could be open and seeing your first client within a week."

Seem impossible? Here's a how-to.

Day 1:

You go to Godaddy.com and register "Counselingby[MyName].com." You subscribe to GoDaddy's web hosting and "Website Builder" DIY services. You browse through pre-made website templates and choose colors for your site. Even though you don't have any technical experience, you find that a little patience (and reading the instructions) gets the job done.

(Don't go it alone: Open your own Thriveworks Counseling Practice!)

You create 10 pages for your new website, each related to a service you provide. You create a page for couples counseling, anxiety therapy, depression therapy, and an "about me" page (to name a few).

You write a thoughtful description of your services on each respective page and email the site to a friend for proofreading. Your friend emails back almost immediately saying "It looks great!" You re-read your pages and find typos everywhere. You fix them.

You post your cell phone number prominently at the top of every page with the promise "Call for a free 10-minute consult."

The website is live! It's clearly a DIY job, but it looks good.

Time to complete: 4 hours.

You need to get your website seen by potential clients. You go to "Google Adwords" and follow the prompts for creating an online advertisement. You remember you have a coupon for $100 in free advertising. While making your first ad you get confused. You are shocked to notice that Google offers free telephone support. The representative helps you post your first Google Ad.

> *"Next, you go to Psychology Today's therapist directory, upload a headshot and write a bio, and begin your 6-month free trial membership."*
>
> *"You can't believe it. In just one day you're already on the web!"*

You login to Facebook and post a status update telling your friends that you're on a mission to open a counseling practice, and see your first client, in only 7 days. You include a link to your new website. Your friends congratulate you! They say they know people to refer. A counselor comments on your post, "Is that ethical?" You consider un-friending him.

Time to complete: 3 hours

Day 2:

You need office space. You search Craigslist and find several health-oriented groups in your area that are looking to rent or share rooms. You respond to the ads by phone (reach voicemails) and by sending emails expressing your interest.

You let your friends and family know that you're looking for a temporary office where you can begin seeing clients. They say they will let you know if they "think of anything." You call Regus®, and they offer you space. The price is $700 per month for a single office, which is more than you want to spend. You tell them that you'll keep it in mind.

Time to complete: 3 hours

In the meantime, you begin compiling all the necessary paperwork you'll need to provide to clients. You ask old professors and colleagues if they have sample intake forms, confidentiality forms, HIPAA privacy policy forms, consent to treat minor children forms, etc. You get a slew of files by email, by surfing the web, and you also reference a textbook from graduate school that includes sample forms. With some adjustments, the forms work well.

Time to complete: 3 hours

You create a Facebook and Twitter account for your practice. You adjust the account settings so that you can post updates to both accounts at once. You plan to write frequent articles on mental health problems, but for now you're going to tell the story of your practice. You take pictures and videos of your day-to-day progress, and post them.

Time to complete: 2 hours

Day 3:

Someone from Craigslist calls you back. You visit the space and find that it's fully furnished. However, the room is only available in the mornings, Friday afternoons, and Saturdays.

A friend, who is an accountant, tells you that he has a 10x12 office that he's not using. You'll need to furnish it, but you'll have access whenever you need it. You sense that running a counseling office out of an accounting firm isn't ideal, but it'll get the job done.

You go to a local furniture store and purchase a couch and a chair for $550 (they will deliver later in the week). You drive to Ikea and spend another $300 on a desk, rug, and some accessories.

You head back to your new office to un-box and assemble your desk. As you look down at the pieces strewn across the floor you wonder if you've made a terrible mistake with your life.

You assemble the desk and arrange the rest of the Ikea items. You feel better. The space doesn't look half bad!

While cleaning up Styrofoam and cardboard, a number you don't recognize appears on your phone. A woman says she found you online. She wants to know if you can accept her insurance. You tell her that you hope to take insurance in the future but you don't now. You ask her if she has out-of-network benefits (she doesn't). You ask her is she'd be willing to pay out-of-pocket if you could offer a price she could afford. She thanks you but says that she needs to think about it.

You make a mental note to apply to Blue Cross, United, Aetna, Cigna, and Tri-care. You know it's going to take much longer than 7 days to get on insurance panels. You decide to start the process next week.

Time to complete: 9 hours

Day 4:

You don't have a logo, or a brand name, or a Limited Liability Company (LLC), or even a sole proprietorship.

While you can put off the logo, you call your accountant friend and ask him what you must do to "register the business." Per his advice, you make a trip to a municipal building and register "[My Name] Counseling" as a sole proprietorship with the city. You pay an $8 fee. A couple next to you is getting their marriage license and talking about pre-marital counseling. You consider telling them about your services but lose your nerve. You make a mental note to "add pre-marital counseling" to your website.

Time to complete: 3 hours

You want a business card and a brochure. Vistaprint looks good and cheap, but you need materials fast. You create a simple business card and brochure using software you already had on your laptop (who knew?). You drive to Staples and they print your brochures.

> *"The woman behind the desk convinces you not to print and cut your own business cards. You thank her for the tip."*

That evening, another unknown number appears on your phone. The caller saw your online ad. He doesn't have insurance, or money. He's looking for free counseling. You speak with him for a few minutes, making sure that he's not in an emergency situation. You then refer him to a local community health center. He thanks you and says he will call.

Time to complete: 3 hours

You log on to Google Adwords and review the data. You're spending $2.13 on average "per click," and you've received 15 clicks to your website. You've spent $31.95 in about 3 days. While still within the $100 coupon, you note that advertising could get expensive fast. You start to panic and wonder if you're in over your head, and if you need more education or supervision. You call an old supervisor and talk it through. You hang your license on the wall and feel slightly more bonafide, ten minutes later you decide no one is ever going to schedule. You call your mom. She believes in you.

Time to complete: 2 hours

Day 5:

You wait half a day for the furniture to be delivered. It arrives and looks amazing! You realize that the overhead lighting won't cut it and you steal two lamps from your apartment. You also steal an alarm clock radio to use as a sound machine.

The little things in setting up the office feel never-ending. Hanging pictures, another trip to staples to get light bulbs, a printer (for intake docs), printer paper, clip boards, pens, organizers, etc.

Time to complete: 8 hours

Day 6:

You hand out brochures to everyone you know, and even visit other local health practices. You call your friends to tell them (gently) to hurry up with those referrals.

Time to complete: 4 hours

You go to Best Buy and purchase a Square® brand credit card reader. You download the Square app and create an account. You can now accept client credit cards. To test the system, you run and charge your own card. Noticing that you just paid a fee to run your own card, you chuckle because you just became your first therapy client. You think to yourself, "how appropriate."

> *"Another unknown number on your phone! You answer. It's the person who called you on day 3. She says that nobody else has answered her calls or called her back, and she's willing to pay out-of-pocket. You schedule an appointment for tomorrow."*

You go online and announce that your practice has its first client on the books! An hour later, you get another call (this one a referral from a friend) and schedule a second client.

Time to complete: 4 hours

Day 7:

Your client shows up for her first appointment. It's after hours, so the office suite is quiet and private.

The client doesn't seem to mind that you're operating out of an accounting firm. In fact, she comments on how easy it was to find the office. She says she loves how you decorated. You play it cool.

As your first session unfolds you realize that you're both going to be fine.

201: Building a Private Practice

Lesson 12:
Match: How to Find the Right Clients for Your Practice

Letting the Right Ones In

When you start a practice, you need clients in the door. Whether you'll stay in business—perhaps whether you'll be able to buy groceries—depends on this. In these times, you could be tempted to push your level of training or competency to its limits.

A client will ask: *"Can you help somebody with bipolar disorder?"*
And you'll say: *"I've worked with clients who've had various depressive disorders."*
A client will ask: *"Can you help me with my panic attacks?"*
And you'll say: *"I've worked with clients struggling with a variety of anxiety issues."*

A client will present night terrors, vaginismus, narcolepsy or something you've never even heard of, and you'll try to find some way to justify your general counseling experience as competency to help that client. What's more, you'll stay late at the office to help a taxi driver who can only come in at midnight. You'll help a client who pays cash, but won't give you his real name.

You might start to feel like the Statue of Liberty — bring me your huddled masses (because it feels wrong to turn away someone in need)! Until, that is, you realize it's killing you — and it's no picnic for your clients either.

A Two-Way Selection

Acquiring clients' needs to be a two-way interview process. The company "Big Ass Fans" knows this. They create some incredible products, and employ more than 200 workers (making them sixth among the top 10 private manufacturers in the US), but they're not trying to appeal to everyone. They know their off-color name means that some people won't do business with them (in fact, they have a collection of angry voicemails from persons telling them as much).

That's okay; the customers they do acquire are a better fit for their company. Persons who offend easily know from square one that they're best to find another fan manufacturer.

> *"While I'm not recommending you name your practice 'Big Ass Counseling,' making your identity clear means that you're going to acquire clients who are consistently a better fit for your practice."*

At our practices — even though we're in the same community as other mental health centers (we now have nearly 20 locations between Cambridge, Massachusetts, and Austin, Texas), accept the same insurance plans and provide similar clinical services — our counselors consistently report that our clients are qualitatively different from clients they've served at other outpatient practices.

The reason? **Our clients are reliably a good fit for outpatient psychotherapy, especially our flavor of outpatient psychotherapy**.

Below are some never-before-revealed processes that we believe influence the type of client who selects our services, and the type of client who self-selects not to purchase our services.

A Clinical Fit

Clinically, if we're not sure a client is a good fit, we tell the client! Then we refer. Too many counseling practices take a "this might be outside our scope, but let's give it a shot anyway" approach, and often it's a terrible fit for both the client and the practice.

This isn't to say that practices mislead clients into choosing them. When a client calls for an appointment, he or she wants to schedule that appointment!

For example, we had a situation where a client wanted someone who specialized in sleep disorders and was available on Tuesday evenings. While we had a sleep disorder specialist on staff, she didn't have openings on Tuesdays. Per the client's adamant request, we reluctantly scheduled him with a very experienced general counselor. While the session seemed to go well, soon after the appointment the client wrote a negative online review because — you guessed it — he felt that the counselor didn't know enough about his sleep disorder!

We refunded his money. We apologized. We tried to refer him. Four years later, that negative review remains.

"Bad for the client. Bad for us."

A Culture Fit

We also have some administrative processes that influence the type of clients who schedule a first session.

1. Credit Card Deposit

To confirm a first session, every new client needs to place a credit card or bankcard on file as a deposit. We see this as a reasonable benchmark to determine a person's seriousness about coming for the session.

We used to have a "hazing" process for new schedulers. In his (or her) first week, he would receive a call from a potential new client who would say that she (or he) didn't "feel comfortable" giving a credit card over the phone. The scheduler would plead, "The person promises she's going to show for the session, and I believe her!" We'd allow the appointment to be scheduled, and *with nearly 100 percent accuracy the client would no-show.*

2. Consent for No-show Fee

When it comes to our late cancellation and no-show fee, we don't just get signed consent — we get true understanding and agreement from clients. We tell clients that the day will likely come when their kid get sick, their car breaks down or they need to work late, and if they don't give us at least 24 hours' notice, we're charging them! There are no freebies.

We've had clients walk out before beginning their first session because they felt the policy was too strict. *That's okay.* It's better we and the client realize that it's not a good fit at the beginning than proceed and later there be hard feelings when the client starts missing sessions.

(NOTE: we've had some of those same clients come back later, okay with the terms, after realizing they prefer our standard of care to our competitors.)

3. Required Information

On the first call, prospective clients need to provide schedulers a considerable amount of information, including their address, insurance card number, date of birth and a few other demographic qualifiers. This is necessary for us to confirm benefits before the first session. This process takes too long for some callers, however, who opt not to schedule.

We don't know exactly how that affects the selection bias of clients who use our service, but we suspect it makes a positive impact.

4. Family Can't Schedule for You

Even if a family member is willing to pay cash in advance (unless it's for a minor child) we don't touch this type of situation. *It gets messy, fast.*

The adult child, spouse or friend attends the first session, but loathes the fact that he/she is there — and doesn't continue. Or the client chooses not to attend, and the payer demands a refund. One way or another, it wastes everyone's time.

5. Being Unapologetically Us

When a client calls our company, every 15 seconds there's a recording that says. "We hate being on hold as much as you do," and then gives the caller the ability to hang up and have us call them back when it's their turn in queue (the total wait is usually under one minute).

Every once in a while, I'll have a scheduler run into my office and say, "Anthony, we just lost a client because of that message! They said they would NEVER go to a counseling practice that uses the word 'HATE'!"

And I'll say: *"That's okay. We use the word hate sometimes. If that's a deal breaker, then it's good fortune that the potential client got to learn that about us early."*

It's Not About Making a Sale, It's about Starting a Relationship

Many people first try to "make the sale" or "schedule the session," and only later begin to discuss terms, conditions, boundaries or fine print. This, of course, leads to a certain number of problem relationships.

> *"Building a practice isn't about getting clients in the door; it's about getting the right clients in the door - ones where there is a mutual good fit for the practice and the client."*

Lesson 13:
Ouch! 17 Reasons Your Insurance Claims Were Denied

Medical billing is a frustrating process for counselors who are often juggling too many business tasks, as well as trying to provide excellent clinical care. In fact, many counseling practices collect less than 85% of the monies that they're rightly owed from insurance companies. However, with good planning, and a smart billing staff (in house or otherwise), your practice can reasonably expect to collect between 96-99% of claims.

Look out for these pitfalls! There are many reasons that claims can go unpaid, including:

You Waited too Long to File the Claim

The vast majority of insurance companies allow 90 days from the time of service to file a claim. However, some insurance companies allow only 30 days to file (and a very few, such as Medicare, allow a year—wow). When claims are filed too long after the date of service, they are rejected.

The Insurance Company Lost the Claim, and then the Claim Expired

Sometimes insurance companies misplace claims. If a misplaced claim doesn't make it into the insurance company's system before the deadline, the claim will be denied. Frustrated providers might find themselves talking to someone from the insurance company who says, "even though the error might have been on our end, there's nothing we can do. The timeframe for filing has expired."

You Lacked Preauthorization / Authorization

Preauthorization is a must for many insurance plans. Provide services without the proper authorization, and the claim will be rejected.

The Patient Didn't acquire a Referral from a Physician

Some insurance plans require not just authorization, but a referral from the patient's primary care provider (PCP) before services can be rendered. Provide services before a referral is confirmed by the insurance company, and the claim will be denied.

You Provided Two Services in One Day

With behavioral health, insurance companies have a strict "one service per day" policy. This means that even if a patient is authorized for 12 sessions of therapy, if you provide two sessions in one day, you won't be paid for the second session. Clinicians who provide group therapy, psychological testing, or medication reviews beware—sometimes these services also fall under the one service per day policy.

You Ran Out of Authorized Sessions

When authorization is granted, it is for a limited number of services / appointments. Lose track of how many appointments were approved for, or how many sessions you have provided, and you might find that you've provided sessions you won't get paid for.

The Authorization Timed Out

In addition to authorizations being for a specific number of sessions, they are also for a specific duration of time. Sometimes the timeframe is as short as 30 days. Provide services after the authorization expires, and your claim will be denied.

The Patient Changed His or Her Insurance Plan

If a patient changes his or her insurance plan, you will need to (a) be a provider networked in the new plan, and (b) get new preauthorization to see the patient / client. Fail to do either of these actions prior to providing services, and your claim will be denied.

The Patient Lost His or Her Insurance Coverage

If a patient loses his or her insurance coverage, your claim will be denied. This is not always evident, as some patients don't know that they have lost their benefits, or may fail to inform you.

The Patient was Late to pay Their COBRA

COBRA is a government program where individuals can keep their health insurance after losing their job. However, those individuals need to pay 100 percent of the policy principle (a lot of money for someone out of work!). If a patient is behind on their COBRA payments, your claim could be denied.

You Sent the Claim to the Wrong Managing Company

Insurance companies often delegate the management of some of their plans, or some services within plans (such as behavioral health) to other companies. Fail to realize this, and send a claim to anyone other than the managing company, and your claim could be denied.

The Provider isn't Paneled with the Insurance Company

If a provider sees a patient, but isn't a paneled provider with the patient's insurance company, the claim will be denied. This sounds like common sense, but with insurance companies merging, and having multiple panels within a single company (e.g., HMO, PPO, etc.), this happens somewhat frequently. Also, if a provider was working for a larger clinic, he (or she) might think that he is a paneled provider, when really he was working under his old employer's contract with the insurance company.

Services Were Rendered at the Wrong Location

When a counselor is paneled with an insurance company, they list one (or multiple) practice addresses. It is important to make sure that providers have all the places they serve patients registered with all the insurance companies they work with. Provide services at an unregistered location, and the claim could be denied.

The Client's Out-of-network Benefits Differ from In-network Benefits

Out-of-network benefits often differ from in-network benefits. For example, with out-of-network benefits, insurance companies often place a greater amount of the payment responsibility on the patient, including the potential for additional deductibles that need to be met. Fail to identify the actual amount owed by the patient for out-of-network services, and you may never receive payment for your work.

The Service was Already Rendered

With Behavioral health, insurance often covers an intake appointment (90801) only once per 3 month (or 1 year) period. Depending on the plan, if your client went to see a therapist prior to you, and the previous therapist billed a 90801, your claim could be denied.

The Patient has an Out-of-State Insurance Plan

If your patient has an out-of-state insurance plan, even if the company is a company that you are networked with, you might find that your reimbursement rate is less, and (depending on the patient's specific plan) your claims can even be denied.

The Patient Has an Unmet Deductible

Even if the patient's insurance card says that their co-pay is $10, if he or she has not met their deductible, you might receive $0 from the insurance company when you file your claim. In addition, be on high alert in January, when deductibles often reset!

While there are pitfalls to look out for when working with insurance companies, being networked with insurance companies can help you build a full caseload of paying clients. In addition, the typical client today has insurance with mental health benefits, and expects to be able to use them when seeing their counselor. Are you ready to evolve with the changes?

Lesson 14:

Setting Admin Fees: Records Requests, Court Appearances & More

Janet has a full roster of clients. She schedules 35 sessions a week, which means that she's busy, but her workload is manageable and she feels well compensated for her efforts. However, lately Janet's been receiving client requests that are leading her to work overtime. Three clients, who are each going through a divorce, have asked for copies of their clinical records to be mailed to their attorneys. One client, who has been missing his college classes, has asked her to write a letter to the registrar confirming his depression diagnosis, treatment, and that his symptoms could be inhibiting his school performance. On top of all that, Janet needs to testify in court next week in regards to a client's child custody case.

With all these requests, Janet knows she's headed toward burnt out. Also, even though she is working more, she's now making *less* money because she's had to cut back on her client sessions to accommodate the administrative demands.

Your Practice

What happens when a client makes a request for her clinical record, asks for a treatment summary, asks for a letter, or perhaps even subpoenas you to testify in court?

Too often, counselors don't have policies in place for handling such requests. Hence, when they occur, they don't always know what to charge, or if they should! Without publishing fees for ancillary services, providers can feel pressured to work for free when clients request services above and beyond their therapy sessions.

Records Requests

Of all the administrative requests clients can make, a request for clinical records is the most regulated when it comes to fees. Under the Health Insurance Portability and Accountability Act (HIPAA), a covered entity can charge reasonable cost-based fees for providing medical records to patients (45 CFR 164.524(c)). In addition, many states have published guidelines for what constitutes "reasonable" fees (you can find state-by-state guidelines at http://thriveworks.com/blog/record-request-fees). For example, Georgia's most recent regulations are as follows:

- A charge of up to $25.88 may be collected for administrative costs. In addition;
- A fee, not to exceed $9.70, for certifying the medical records may also be charged. In addition;
- The cost of postage may also be charged. In addition;
- Fees for copying documents may be:
- $0.97 per page for the first 20 pages
    1. $0.83 per page for pages 21 through 100
    2. $0.66 for each page copied in excess of 100 pages
- For medical records that are not in paper form, the provider shall be entitled to recover the full reasonable cost of reproduction.

In contrast, Massachusetts' regulations specify for allowable rates:

- A $19.84 base charge for clerical expenses. In addition;
- A fee to cover the actual cost of postage. In addition;
    1. $0.67 per page charge for the first 100 pages copied; and
    2. $0.35 per page charge for each page in excess of 100 pages.

While many state-specified fees will cover the costs of practices with administrative staff, the low rates are a tough pill to swallow for solo-providers, who are taking a drastic pay cut for any time spent producing medical records and *not* seeing clients.

Writing a Treatment Summary

At times a client might ask for a treatment summary. In contrast to a records request, the cost of producing a treatment summary is at the discretion of the provider.

Writing a Letter

Your attorney will always write you a letter. You want him/her to write a letter to your grandma, demanding that her meatloaf be less spicy, and cooked longer? Sure! Your attorney will write it. It will cost you, but he/she will write it.

I recently met with a clinician who experienced a situation wherein a client—during her third session—requested a letter detailing that her depression was inhibiting her ability to attend class. She responded that she would only write a letter if the client was in treatment for at least two months, responding, "we're not a letter writing service."

When I spoke with this clinician in more detail, I found that there were two specific reasons for her reluctance. First, her office had no rates in place for this type of task. Therefore, every time she would write a letter, it would be gratis. She wanted to reserve these time-consuming "special favors" for long-term clients.

Second, she felt that such a letter would be in support of the client's assertion that her depression was the cause of her truancy. While she agreed that the client was depressed, she wasn't comfortable writing a letter that drew a firm causal relationship.

Issue one is easily solved by publishing fees for letter writing. Wisconsin–based counselor Kendall Crook charges $37-$150 for documents, varying by document type (records requests are $0.31 per page, plus postage). These fees are presented to clients during their first appointment, as part of their larger fee agreement. Regarding his rates, Kendall says "We [his practice] use templates, which saves time, so we're able to charge less. Depending on the nature of the letter, we can usually complete the project within 30 minutes. While the reason for the fee isn't to deter patients, once clients hear that there is a fee, they consider whether they actually need the document they're requesting."

Second, counselors' letters can be descriptive, not interpretive. Using the example above, a letter could say, "Client X has participated in three sessions of counseling with me. During these sessions she has reported trouble waking up in the morning, feelings of despair, and a difficulty completing everyday tasks. She reports that her symptoms are making it difficult for her to attend class. Following the guidelines of the DSM-IV, I have diagnosed Client X as having Major Depressive Disorder."

How to determine price?

It is reasonable to charge for the time it takes to compose documents, plus any postage fees incurred. However, this does not mean a provider needs to charge by the hour. It may be wise for providers to simply charge a flat rate that includes all costs. This helps to avoid a client conflict such as, "Did this really take you X minutes?" and (more likely) to avoid self-conflict such as, "This took me an hour. Did it take me longer than it should have? I'm a slow typist—should I really charge for this? Did this envelope need four stamps?"

When setting rates, counselors should consider the actual amount of time they will need to complete such a task. Note that one's "actual" time might be double the ideal amount of time (put simply, something that you think should take 20 minutes, will probably take 40). In addition, counselors should consider what level of financial remuneration will make completing various administrative tasks a positive and rewarding experience. Providers should not feel pressure to charge less to produce documents than they make in therapy (BTW, my attorney will charge his full fee whether he's providing expert legal advice or checking my spelling). In fact, it isn't unreasonable for providers to charge above their usual therapy rates, as they are providing a special service.

Attendance in Court

Texas-based counselor Todd Daehnert, states in a document to his clients titled *Court Action/Legal Fees*, "Clients are discouraged from having their therapist subpoenaed...Even though you are responsible for the testimony fee, it does not mean that my testimony will be solely in your favor. I can only testify to the facts of the case and to my professional opinion." For those who fail to heed counselor Todd's discouragement, the following fees are in effect:

1. Preparation time (including submission of records): $220/hr
2. Phone calls: $220/hr
3. Depositions: $250/hour
4. Time required in giving testimony: $250/hour
5. Mileage: $0.40/mile
6. Time away from office due to depositions or testimony: $220/hour
7. All attorney fees and costs incurred by the therapist as a result of the legal action.
8. Filing a document with the court: $100
9. The minimum charge for a court appearance: $1500

A retainer of $1500 is due in advance. If a subpoena or notice to meet attorney(s) is received without a minimum of 48-hour notice there will be an additional $250 "express" charge. Also, if the case is reset with less than 72 business hours' notice, then the client will be charged $500 (in addition to the retainer of $1500).

Finally, all fees are doubled if counselor Todd had scheduled plans to go out of town.

I spoke with counselor Todd, who has appeared in court over 40 times in the last 7 years, mostly for child custody cases. According to Todd, "The first couple times I appeared for clients I didn't charge. Then I thought, 'I'm never doing that again.'" Todd began charging his usual therapy rate of $115 an hour, "...but I didn't want to go. I'd rather make less money and not be at court all day." To make it worth his time, he raised his rates to where they are now. Todd explains, "Clients are paying thousands, or tens of thousands, of dollars [for their case]. They don't balk at my fee. It's worth every dime."

Honest and Fair

Administrative fees are not the "hidden fees" of seeing a therapist. They are honest and fair charges for additional services that clients may want. Post your fee schedule in your office. Include it with clients' intake paperwork. Good clients will understand why these charges exist, and respect that counselors need to charge for their time.

Lesson 15:
Focus: How to Specialize Your Practice

A question I'm often asked by counselors is whether they should specialize. That is, should they focus their counseling practice in a specific area? It's a hard question to answer, as even successful business people disagree. In this lesson, I'll describe four ways that counselors can specialize, and offer some insights into how specializing can help (or hurt) a counseling practice.

There are four areas in which counseling practices can specialize:

1. Populations Served
2. Problems Treated
3. Treatment Methods Used
4. Business Practices.

Each is described below.

1) Populations Served

Children, couples, firefighters, Mormons, Texans, criminals, and Texan criminals: Specializing in a client population means limiting one's practice to serving a group with an identifying characteristic other than the presenting problem.

This type of specialization is most successful when members of the population are known to limit their search to counselors who work specifically with their population. For example, many Christians will refuse to see a counselor that does not identify him- or herself as a "Christian counselor." Similarly, executives, GLBTQ clients, and many ethnic groups will seek out therapists with specific expertise in helping persons in their population.

The downside of specializing in a specific population is that one limits their potential client base. A colleague of mine had a website with a header that said, "The Child and Adolescent Experts." While the specialization helped the practice win both school and court contracts (working with delinquent adolescents), the practice still struggled because the local demand for child therapy was too small. As soon as they expanded their practice to encompass families and couples, their business grew.

Broadening (or diluting) their specialization worked for them. However, it's also weakened their grip on the child and adolescent market. Since they're no longer marketing themselves as "the child and adolescent experts," other practices in town are more able to compete for those clients.

2) Problems Treated

From Social Anxiety Disorder to substance abuse, there is no shortage of psychological problems and life issues in which to specialize.

Specializing in a specific problem is more than simply adding an item to a practice's menu of disorders treated. It takes commitment to limit one's practice to a specific problem—and both clients and colleagues tend to respect counselors willing to focus. Moreover, if you choose a problem that the average clinician finds difficult or undesirable, such as severe mental illnesses, autism spectrum disorders, or high-risk clients, the specialization should help to encourage peer-referrals.

Alternatively, if you brand your practice as "the depression specialist," peer-referrals will likely be sparse. Still, you will gain the attention of potential clients with depression, who may look favorably upon the practice built specifically for their presenting problem.

3) Treatment Methods Used

Treatment methods can include psychoanalysis, Eye Movement Desensitization and Reprocessing (EMDR), Dialectical Behavioral Therapy (DBT), positive psychology, and many more. Specializing in a method of treatment is a good way to recruit the savvy client who knows the type of treatment he/she wants. However, the average client is rarely focused on treatment method.

I often see counselors excited about their EMDR certifications; but less often do I see those certifications become the genesis of a thriving practice. Conversely, I have known of a tight knit community of psychoanalysists who refer within their circles, and seem to have a loyal following of psychoanalysis-seeking clients.

In my own clinical work, rarely (but sometimes) do clients seek me out because of my counseling methodology. Hence, from a business perspective, while there often isn't a big upside to specializing in a treatment method, there probably isn't a huge downside either.

4) Business Practices

Walk in appointments, phone or video sessions, at home therapy, 24-hour customer service, high prices, low prices, intern-level counselors: The business decisions that make up a practice's unique brand identity are limited only by the founder's imagination (and resources).

But can business practices be a specialization? Yes! If every session is $600, and you offer caviar to your clients, your practice specializes in providing a high-priced, first-class, counseling experience (ok, that's debatable, but you get the point). If sessions are $40 and lack frills, you specialize in providing an economic counseling option, much like Southwest provides low cost airfare.

Which identity to choose? Customer service is in demand right now, as recent polls show that most consumers are willing to pay more for goods and services in exchange for a great buying experience. Also, some business practices are evergreen—such as affordability and convenience (No one is ever going to say, "I wish this service cost more, and was harder to use."). Still, to really set your practice apart, clients need an experience that is delightful, memorable, and unique.

Specialization Tips

Below are seven tips based on my experience working with counselors starting new practices.

1) Don't specialize in Group Therapy

Some counselors, starting out, think that offering group therapy will help them build a caseload. Nothing could be further from the truth. Instead, groups tend to work best when a practice has an over-abundance of incoming clients who want help. For example, a group is a good option if your practice is receiving a never-ending influx of clients who are court-mandated to receive anger management.

2) Avoid Creating a Holistic Health Program

A counselor starting a private practice might get the idea to begin a holistic health program. These programs are usually counseling combined with some number of ancillary services such as yoga, exercise, nutrition, meditation, massage, etc. In addition, they often require some type of upfront commitment from the client to participate. The idea is that by taking a "whole health" approach to care, the practice will become differentiated in the marketplace, and also be more helpful to the clients than psychotherapy alone. However, such programs create a barrier for building a practice, because most prospective clients don't want to sign up for a program, they just want to try out a normal counseling session.

3) Consider Demand

Before selecting a specialty, try to determine if there is enough demand for what you are offering. Tony Hsieh, CEO of Zappos, states, "In business, one of the most important decisions for an entrepreneur or a CEO to make is what business to be in. It doesn't matter how flawlessly a business is executed if it's the wrong business or if it's in too small a market. Imagine if you were the most efficient manufacturer of seven-fingered gloves. You offer the best selection, the best service, and the best prices for seven-fingered gloves—but if there isn't a big enough market for what you sell, you won't get very far."

4) Stay Consistent

Don't jump ship on an idea that's working. In *The 22 Immutable Laws of*

Branding, authors Ries and Ries write, "Consistency built the Little Caesars brand, and lack of consistency is in the process of destroying the Little Caesars brand. "Pizza! Pizza!" became the chain's rallying cry. Where else could you get two pizzas for the price of one? The power of this branding program made Little Caesars the second-largest pizza chain in America. "Why should we limit ourselves to take-out pizza only?" the bored executives asked. So Little Caesars introduced "Delivery. Delivery." And promptly fell to third place in sales, after Pizza Hut and Domino's Pizza.

It gets worse. In order to turn the chain around, Little Caesars went big. The small pizza became a medium-size pizza. The medium-size pizza became a large pizza. And the large pizza became an extra-large pizza. Talk about confusion.

"I'd like to order a medium-size pizza, please."

"Do you want a Pizza Hut medium, which is actually our small size? Or do you want a Little Caesars medium, which is actually a Pizza Hut large?"

"Uh . . . do I still get two pizzas for the price of one?"

"Pizza! Pizza!? No, we don't do that anymore."

A pity. Little Caesars had one of the best brands in the pizza category. The only brand focused on takeout. The only brand with an identity and a message. (Pizza! Pizza!) And now it has nothing."

5) Be the best in the world

In order to have a truly great practice, you need to be best in the world. Sound overwhelming? Don't worry; this can be both highly focused and location-specific. For example, you could be the best at "providing counseling to single mothers in central Virginia" or "providing CBT to undergraduate students attending Virginia Tech." When potential clients are looking for a counselor, they are looking for the best option in their world. That is, the best counselor within a few miles, under their budget, who has openings on Thursdays or Saturdays. Jim Collins elaborates, "We confront the brutal facts of what we can—and equally cannot—become the best in the world at, and we do not allow bravado to obscure the truth." Of what can you be the best in the world? Of what can you not?

6) Take a flyer

If you have a new, creative idea for your practice, but are not sure if it will work—give it a try! Don't bet the farm on the idea, but don't play the game so safe that you never take any chances. When starting a practice, a lot of what you do is going to be like throwing handfuls grass into the air and seeing if it catches the wind. Most will just fall to the ground, but every once in a while something will catch air—and take off!

7) Specialization can work in a small town, too

I used to think that in order to succeed in a small city or town, a counseling practice would need to offer broad and general services. However, this isn't always the case. While there are less people, there may also be fewer clinicians. This past year, I spent a lot of time in a small city. Residents are paying big city prices to meet with the few counselors who are known to be good at couples' therapy, or eating disorders. Supply and demand works in small towns, too.

Lesson 16:
Why the Life Coach is Eating the Counselor's Lunch!

Life coaches have seemingly done a bit of magic, making dollars appear out of thin air. And everyone's thrilled, except for counselors, who are patting their jacket pockets and asking, "Where's my wallet?" Here's how the trick is done.

First, remove stigma

Some years ago, persons experienced in sports coaching and motivational speaking began to transition into the one-on-one helping business.

In 1974, W. Timothy Gallwey wrote The Inner Game of Tennis: The Classic Guide to the Mental Side of Peak Performance. Many consider this to be the first major transition from sports coaching into personal coaching. The text, borrowing from humanistic and transpersonal psychological principles, addresses the concept of "the opponent within" and outlines a model for self-improvement that could be applied to a broad spectrum of life situations.

Thomas Leonard, founder of the International Coach Federation, is credited for coining the term life coaching. Although some contend that the name was created to avoid regulated terms such as counseling and psychotherapy, the rebranding offers an advantage. That is, by presenting something different than "counseling," life coaches achieved a feat that has eluded counselors for decades — they took the stigma out of seeking help.

Second, claim dominance in a new category

The Blue Ocean Strategy is a business strategy wherein a new product or service category is created next to a previously existing category. The goal is to eliminate the competition by creating something new. To create a blue ocean, one must:

- Raise: Offer something more than the industry standard
- Reduce: Offer something less than the industry standard
- Create: Offer something never offered in the industry
- Eliminate: Remove something usually offered in the industry

For example, at a time when many wine companies were competing to offer the most sophisticated and complex wine, the brand Yellow Tail created a blue ocean by offering:

- No jargon (eliminate)
- No importance on aging (eliminate)
- Less selection: one red, one white (reduce)
- A simple, modern bottle label (create)
- Sweeter than usual wine that is easy to drink (raise/create)
- A low price point/higher value (raise)

Life coaches, using Blue Ocean Strategy, don't offer help with psychological problems or emotional disorders. Rather, they specialize in helping normal people excel in life. Life coaches explain, "Counselors can get you from unwell to neutral (that is, from -10 to 0); life coaches can move you from neutral to peak performance (from 0 to +10)!" This message is appealing to persons who don't want to be identified with a "clinical problem." It also makes counselors look less competent at growth-focused care.

Third, manufacture credibility

Credibility is added to a field by establishing professional organizations and certifications. For example, the International Coach Federation offers three levels of certification, each of which require training, testing and documented coaching hours. The certifications look professional and polished (the 2,500 hours needed to become a "master coach" appear equivalent to what licensed counselors need to acquire after earning their master's degree), but upon deeper investigation, the qualitative differences in academic rigor are extensive.

Life coaches have been so effective at claiming expertise that even licensed counselors sometimes wonder, "Am I missing something?" In fact, I often encounter counselors who have enrolled in life coaching certification programs themselves.

One of my employees, an excellent counselor named Deborah Brigandi, recently attended a life coaching conference in Boston. Reportedly, the sessions taught basic counseling techniques, renamed and repackaged, without background. She told me, "It's as if they read the CliffNotes from a counseling program. Every topic addressed was oversimplified, and they didn't see that they were oblivious to vast amounts of knowledge and research."

Life coaches often say that they partner with licensed counselors, so Deborah was surprised by what she observed at the conference. "They were really negative toward counseling," she said. "I was really disappointed!"

Shine a light on life coaching

If counselors can communicate the truth about the life coaching industry, they can reclaim territory that has been lost to life coaches. Here are two thoughts:

1) Show what life coaches lack. Counselors need to communicate to the public the low amount of training and education necessary to hang a shingle as a life coach. For example, I can envision job ads that contrast the qualification requirements for counselors and life coaches:

Become a counselor:

- 6 Years of College Minimum
- 2 Years of Full-time Post-Master's Clinical Work and Supervision
- State-sanctioned Testing for Licensure
- Continuing Education Required

Become a life coach:

- No College Education Required!
- No State License Required!
- Solicit paying clients within weeks!

2) You want the very best life coach? Hire a counselor. Clients are going to continue seeking growth-focused care, and because of that counselors should use the term life coach. Moreover, the professional counselor should be branded as "the original" life coach.

My practice in Cambridge, MA is called ***Thrive Boston Counseling and Life Coaching***. Many prospective clients call us and say, "I don't know if I need counseling or life coaching." We reply, "That's not a problem. Our fully licensed counselors are also excellent life coaches." What more could a client want?

Lesson 17:

How to "Wow" Your Clients with Your Counseling Space

As a counselor, your primary focus in on providing great clinical care. This, of course, is the most important thing you can do to help build your counseling practice. However, while great clinical care is necessary, it's not all you need, and many good counselors fail at building a private practice.

In this lesson, I'm going to talk about your counseling office. We'll look at two things:

1) What your competition's office looks like, and
2) What your clients expect your office to look like.

Here's my philosophy on client service: doing a good job might lead to a satisfied client, but what you want isn't just a satisfied client. You want clients so delighted by your service that they can't help but to tell others about their experience. To do this, you need to 'wow' your clients with great care and great service, and the latter includes your professional space.

Your Counseling Office — The Bar is Low!

When I first moved to Cambridge, I worked for a counseling center that literally had not been cleaned for 11 years!! Old, cheap carpets were threadbare and stained, and those stains were covered by more cheap throw rugs. The place had a funky smell, and some of my clients were allergic to the dust. The couch in one office was clearly a relic from the 60's, complete with broken springs. The walls of each therapy room were lined with cheap bookcases with sagging shelves (I later discovered that behind almost every bookshelf was a dead mouse still in a mousetrap). It was disgusting—and, I'll admit, a bit extreme.

While I haven't come across any other counseling office quite as bad as that one, I haven't been impressed by many, either. Walk into your typical counseling office waiting room and you'll see walls painted a dull white or beige, or covered in old wallpaper. If there is art on the walls at all, it's cheap, ugly, and all too often, depressing. The furniture is old. The space is dark. There's no WIFI. The only refreshment available is from a water cooler, with a stack of wax Dixie cups nearby.

As if that isn't bad enough, it's not uncommon for clients to wait in hallways. It's not uncommon for clients to sit just inches from their therapist's office door, and hear the session before theirs going on through the office door.

Because the bar is so low in some cases, you might think that it shouldn't take much to 'wow' clients with your office space, right? WRONG!

Your Counseling Practice Office — The Bar is High!

While counseling offices are often in need of improvement, many clients' perceptions of what a counseling office should be aren't from the offices of other real-life clinicians in town. Nope. Many clients learn about therapy from seeing therapy on TV. And if you haven't noticed, counseling offices on TV are over-the-top amazing!

Ever see the office of Tony Soprano's psychotherapist? It's huge, it's round, and the walls are...is that mahogany?

Have you ever seen the episodes of House M.D. where Dr. Gregory House
meets with his psychiatrist? The space is incredible (the image here doesn't
do it justice). There's a carafe of water on the coffee table (classy), and
they're each sitting in $5,000 designer chairs.

Or, my personal favorite – did you watch the episodes of Nip / Tuck when
Shawn McNamara and Christian Troy went to see a couples' counselor? The
office is 1500 square feet, and they must be on the 30th floor, because the
view of the Los Angeles skyline is breathtaking (I couldn't find a picture, but
check out the shot below of the McNamara / Troy offices in general — wow)!

Gregory House M.D., in therapy.

The waiting room of McNamara / Troy (Note, this is before they opened their really nice office, in Los Angeles.

Tony Soprano, in Therapy.

Therapy office, as portrayed on Mad Men.

How to Wow Clients with your Counseling Space

So, with the bar being set so high on TV, how do you impress your clients with your counseling space? I have found that there are many things that therapists can do to create a fantastic office experience, even if the 'bones' of your space has some shortcomings, and even on a smaller budget. For example, my counseling practice (Thrive Counseling), moved from a 12th floor penthouse office suite with a stunning view of the Boston skyline, to the second floor suite, with no view, in a more industrial building, and our clients LOVED IT!

There are several things that you can do, for little money, to give your clients a wow experience when they enter your counseling space.

Above, I talked about "the counseling office" and how, while it may be true that therapist offices are sometimes poorly designed, client's expectations of what counselor offices should look like are often derived from what they've seen on TV (read the previous post to view images of some fantastic TV counseling offices!).

In this lesson, I'll provide some ideas on how you can make your counseling office a welcoming and impressive space for your clients.

Exceeding Client Expectations

Creating an experience that clients remember and talk about is important to building a thriving practice. When it comes to your office space, one way to do this is to have the most expensive office in town: the best view, the most square feet, and the most lavish and expensive furniture and flooring.

Truly, that's not a bad approach! You'd sure get clients talking. In addition, according to some studies, the better your practice location, the less you'll need to spend on advertising (I believe that came from "The eMyth Revisited," by Michael Gerber; a great book). However, throwing your life savings at your office is just one way to "wow" your clients and create an experience that your clients will talk about.

Here is a list of ideas (most of them we have used at Thriveworks) to create a fantastic counseling space on a budget.

Paint the Pig

Adding color to the walls makes a huge difference to any space, and costs relatively little. At Thriveworks, we had a designer pick out 3 colors that would work with the tan walls that were in the office suite when we moved in. By using multiple colors, we were able to create a great-looking custom paint job, while not even needing to paint every wall (In the end, the walls were 4 colors: tan/beige, light blue, darker blue, and brown).

Don't settle for white or beige walls. A good paint job can entirely change the feel and energy of a space.

Wall Tattoos

Wall tattoos are a quick and inexpensive way to add a ton of design to your office. Check out DaliDecals.com or walltat.com. The modern designs make a fun (and still professional) impression.

Word to the wise, use these sparingly (our designer warned us). Apply decals to a maximum of one wall per room, and not in every room.

Inexpensive, Original Art

Inexpensive, original, art seems to add more depth than the typical framed print.

Mywhitewalls.com offers real painted art at shockingly low prices (hint, there's always a 50% off coupon floating around. I believe the word "Mother" still works as a 50% off coupon code, from a Mother's Day Sale 3 years ago).

At Thrive, we bought a piece of original art for nearly every room, and it really makes an impression. Some of the paintings are great. Some are really ugly–but even the ugly paintings make good conversation pieces.

Have good Lighting

Read my text: No Dark Corners.

Lighting makes a huge impact. Make sure that you have enough lighting options. Avoid "soul draining" fluorescents. We installed Hamilton Bay track lighting (Home Depot brand), and also liberally purchased table lamps, desk lamps, floor lamps, torch lamps, spotlights, and more. We also installed a lot of dimmer switches to make the lighting even more flexible.

Lighting can make or break a room, so be sure to get it right.

Better Sound Machines

Most therapists I know use these brown noise machines that sound like tearing wrapping paper. I hate them. Instead, try this sound machine by Homedics. It has 8 different soothing sounds, and has a better-than-usual volume control switch.

Music

Have music. Good music! At Thriveworks, we have stereos in both our waiting rooms, along with a stack of Yoga CDs and albums of bands the staff likes. When we're sick of music, we play NPR. Clients really seem to like the variety.

A Nice Place to Sit

While you might not want to take out a small business loan on furniture, you do want to have quality furniture.

At Thriveworks, with some trial and error, we were able to find really nice chairs at $200 a piece. We also found a furniture retailer, where we could buy a couch and love seat set (high quality) for about $1300. One set like this is good for two therapy offices, if you split the couch and love seat and accompany them with one or two nice chairs.

No old furniture. No broken furniture. And please, don't over-furnish a room—nothing makes a place feel more claustrophobic than too much furniture.

Magazines

Have lots of magazine subscriptions for both men and women. Subscribe to Inc Magazine, Fast Company, Golf, Sports illustrated, Time, Entertainment Weakly, Simple Living, Martha Stewart Living (a favorite), Health, parenting, GQ (Gentleman's Quarterly), Wired, Parenting, People, Esquire, and maybe a local magazine.

Why so many? Well, why not? It's not expensive (most yearly subscriptions cost under $15 a year!) Remember, your goal is to provide something remarkable to your clients. I bet you'll get some positive comments, if you do this.

In addition, you will want to discard (recycle, that is) any magazines as soon as a corner is bent or a page is torn. At Thrive, sometimes we will throw them out immediately because we don't like the condition in which they arrived.

Cell Phone Charger

Here's something that you can offer that will be a big hit. You can purchase, for about $40, a universal cell-phone charger that can charge every major cell phone on the market.

Your clients will know that you care about them so much, you even want them to be able to charge their cell phones before (or during) their session.

Refreshments

Offer coffee, tea, and hot cocoa at a minimum. We use a top of the line Keurig machine for coffee, offer TAZO tea, and we have a glass-front refrigerator full of name brand sodas.

Also, consider offering candy and chocolate. Does it get expensive?—you bet! However, it's just one more thing that will sets you apart, and will make your clients feel cared for.

WIFI

Have free WIFI! Your clients will thank you for it, and you're probably already paying for Internet. Bonus: Put up a sign asking for some online reviews, and you might get an immediate return on your investment.

More Ideas?

What other ways can you think of to create a counseling space that wows your clients and gets them talking? Share your thoughts at anthony@thriveworks.com!

A therapy room at Thriveworks: Featuring new furniture, wall art, and fresh paint (Cambridge, MA).

Waiting rooms at Thriveworks: Featuring new furniture, wall art, and fresh paint (Top 2 images: Cambridge, MA. Bottom panoramic: Denver, CO).

Thriveworks waiting rooms featuring wall tattoos (Top to bottom:
Lynchburg, VA: Philadelphia, PA: Richmond, VA).

This sound machine, by HoMedics, costs around $20 dollars. The 6 sounds it
offers are a refreshing change from standard "white noise" machines.

A variety of magazines for men and women. Subscriptions to weekly publications are especially useful, as magazines begin to look tattered quickly. Magazines with bent corners are thrown away.

A cell phone charger in every treatment office is a low cost way to show clients you're willing to go the extra mile. This universal charger costs around $30. Unlike years past, where there were 12+ common plugs, you can now get away with the 3 major versions: USB, Micro USB, Apple Lightning Wire.

Lesson 18:
Making Great First Impressions: 9 Practical Tips

If you're like many counselors, much of your day is spent in session. Because of this, a new client's first contact with you often isn't you—it's your voicemail! Does this first impression reflect competence, approachability, and your unique personality?

> *You have reached the confidential voicemail of Joyce Drupal M.A., Licensed Professional Counselor and Certified Alcohol and Drug Counselor. I'm not available right now to take your call, but please leave a message, speaking slowly and clearly, and I will return your call within two business days. If you are experiencing a medical emergency, please hang up and dial 911 or go to your nearest emergency room. If you have an appointment, and are driving to the office, park in the lot behind the building, and not on 5th street where you WILL be ticketed [5 seconds of fumbling as Joyce tries to hang up her phone, and finally...BEEP!].*

Sound Familiar? I make about 50 phone calls to counselors a week, and leave about 49 voicemail messages. While it would be better to reach a live person, the real nuisance is the droning (and dare I say depressing) voicemail messages. They're too often uncreative, uninspired, and at times unprofessional.

Let's raise the bar! Here are some tips for improving counselor voicemail messages.

1) Trim the fat.

Voicemail recordings are too long. Trim them back! Does one need to say, "I'm not available right now to take your call"—isn't that self-evident? Does one need to recite their degrees and certifications, or could a simple "This is counselor John Doe," suffice?

2) Smile.

Smiles are audible! Broadcasters know that smiling when speaking literally changes one's voice—making one sound more positive and energetic. Remember this, and always be smiling when recording an audio message.

3) Provide value.

Try to give something of value. An inspiring quotation, a kind word, or even a well told joke might improve a caller's experience (e.g., "Don't forget to vote today," "In the middle of difficulty lies opportunity" - Albert Einstein, "Happiness is not a place you arrive, but a way of traveling.").

4) Hang up.

When you're finished with your message, end the call. Fumbling to hang up the phone can make one seem incompetent, and might detract from a caller's confidence in the counselor's abilities.

5) Um, Write it out.

Having a script might sound a bit formal, but it helps to avoid those "ums" and "uhs" that can occur when recording. Also, a script will help you keep your message tight. However, you might need to practice reading it through a few times, so that you don't sound stiff.

6) Update daily.

Time-sensitive updates are a double-edged sword. Having a voicemail that says "Today's Tuesday the 1st" can make you appear on top of your game, unless it's Wednesday the 2nd (or, even, Tuesday the 2nd).

7) Consider your emergency instructions.

If your practice offers emergency services, having voice mail instructions on how to access those services may be of value. However, simply telling callers to "dial 911 or go to an emergency room" might be ineffectual.

This week, my staff made calls to the ethics departments of both the American Counseling Association and the American Psychological Association, and representatives' comments were alike: Providers include "call 911" statements to guide clients in crisis, and ethics codes address the issues of both client abandonment and emergency.

The ACA Code of Ethics, in Standard A.11, states "... Counselors assist in making appropriate arrangements for the continuation of treatment, when necessary, during interruptions such as vacations, illness and following termination...When counselors transfer or refer clients to other practitioners, they ensure that appropriate clinical and administrative processes are completed..." In addition, Section A.12.g. states counselors are to "Inform clients of emergency procedures, such as calling 911 or a local crisis hotline, when the counselor is not available."

While this is a matter that can benefit from continued ethical debate, if a counselor discusses emergency procedures with clients during informed consent, there might be no need to restate those procedures on voicemail.

8) Return calls.

Let callers know when you're going to get back with them, and make it as short a time period as possible. If you offer 50-minute sessions, can you return calls between appointments? If so, say, "I return most calls within an hour."

9) Veto Voicemail.

To provide the best client experience, always have someone answer the phone—even if the live attendant can only take a message. There are many answering services available for this. Thriveworks.com (my company) is just one of them, and offers a service called "ThriveAssist," where medical receptionists can take messages, and also confirm, schedule, and change client appointments for counselors.

An Easy Win

Voicemail is low effort, and high impact. Spending a few minutes preparing a quality message can help you to not only make a first impression, but will also serve your clients and your practice for months, or years.

Lesson 19:
Always Be Doing Something Special for Your Clients

"Some call it the 'wow' factor. Others, 'surprise and delight.' Others call it being 'notable.' At Disney, they call it 'plussing' - the act of always adding a little something more to a guest's experience."

A man goes to a restaurant, and at the end of the meal he agrees to take a survey.

The questions are as follows:

1. When you arrived, were you greeted by a host?

Answer: YES

2. Where you seated promptly?

Answer: YES

3. Was your server professional and courteous?

Answer: YES

4. Did your food arrive as you ordered?

Answer: YES

5. Were you satisfied with the quality of your meal?

Answer: YES

6. Was your check/bill correct?

Answer: Yes

7. Would you recommend our restaurant to a friend?

Answer: MAYBE

What went wrong?

Everything seemed to be going so well until the last question! This restaurant did everything right but missed the mark on one important fact: When someone goes out to eat, he/she expects to be seated promptly. He/she expects the food to arrive as ordered. He/she expects the bill to be correct. The restaurant met the customer's expectations, but failed to exceed them.

To have a restaurant, or any business, that is worthy of a customer's recommendation or referral, your business needs to offer something special for your clients. Some call it the "wow" factor. Others, "surprise and delight." Others call it being "notable." At Disney, they call it "plussing" — the act of always adding a little something more to a guest's experience.

What Does Doing Something Special for Your Clients Look Like?

There's a restaurant outside Boston, and at the end of the meal everyone receives a piece of blue cotton candy.

Two things I need to mention about this:

- When you receive a bill at a restaurant, you've just finished a meal and probably also had dessert. The last thing anyone needs is more food.
- I've come to learn that cotton candy is 99 percent air. There's so little substance — it's practically a low calorie food — and costs no more than a standard dinner mint.

How do people respond? The food, service, and ambiance are all exceptional. Still, what everyone talks about is a five-cent piece of cotton candy: "That's so Americana! I haven't had cotton candy in years!" Just mention the neighborhood and people reply, "Have you been to XYZ restaurant; that place that gives cotton candy?"

What About the Counseling?

When I mention the "do something special for your clients" concept to clinicians, a common question is, "Isn't the most important thing the counseling?" *My answer: "Yes!"*

If you're providing a counseling experience that is exceeding your client's expectations, you will have no shortage of clients telling their friends how much they "need to schedule an appointment." In addition, counselors who are charismatic, who invoke an emotional response from their clients or who are unusually effective in driving client change will build demand for their services faster than counselors whose clients don't walk out of their sessions with their worlds rocked.

Some clinicians grow their practices because they are extraordinarily gifted; others are just charming and enigmatic. Whether or not you like Dr. Phil, his charisma made him a blockbuster therapist. Clearly, there are ethical issues here. Even considering whether clinical care could result in referrals presents issues as one's clinical work with a client should be solely focused on the success of that client.

A Moving Target

While excellent clinical care is crucial, one would be remiss not to consider everything a client sees, hears, feels, smells and tastes when interacting with his/her practice. However, the process of "doing something special" is a moving target.

Long ago, we began installing glass-front beverage centers in the waiting rooms of Thriveworks centers, to offer clients free soft drinks. Fast-forward seven years and soft drinks have changed from a whimsical treat to a public health pariah. We then stocked those beverage centers with bottled water until bottled water changed from a luxury item to an environmental catastrophe. We eventually removed the beverage centers.

There was a time when offering Wi-Fi in waiting rooms was exciting. Today, not only is it unimpressive, few clients use it because their cellular data plans and personal hotspots have made the need for it obsolete.

As someone who's always doing something special for your clients, you need to always be asking: "What's next?"

Make A List

Offering something special can be expensive, but doesn't need to be.

Imagine: Every client who visits your office gets their own private waiting area with a reclining leather chair, monitor and individual satellite radio station. Clients can dim, brighten, or change the color of their lighting. The experience is private, personalized and probably out of your budget.

If you're thinking about offering something special for your clients, you'll have lots of ideas — and some will be out of reach.

That's okay; it shows you're exploring lots of options. Also, maybe instead of all the features mentioned above, a simplified offering of reclining leather chairs and privacy dividers IS within your budget.

To start your list, here are some cost effective ideas:

- A late cancellation fee for the counselor. If you cancel a session with less than 24 hours' notice, you pay your client a no-show fee.
- Call every client the day after his/her first session, just to check in.
- Every new client gets a copy of your favorite life improvement book.
- Every client gets a "membership card" containing your direct contact information.

It takes continual effort to always be doing something special for your clients. Your colleagues might think you're eccentric, but your clients will love your practice.

Lesson 20:
Weathering the Slow Summer Slump

Every therapist has heard about the summer slump. That period, mid-year, when kids are out of school, families are on vacation, and nobody is depressed or has any problems at all—and therefore, not in need of counseling. This month, we're going to talk about how to survive those "slow summer months."

1) It's Mostly a Myth

You know how people say that x-disorder is a myth perpetuated by big pharma companies to peddle meds? Well, maybe the "summer slump" is a myth perpetuated by small counseling practices that want to be closed while the swimming pool is open. Okay, so maybe I'm exaggerating (just a little) but before I get a pile of angry emails, hear me out:

- The idea that people aren't depressed in the summer is just plain wrong.
- Yes, kids are out of school, but they're still alive. Meaning, there are still issues to be addressed.
- While people do go on summer vacation, most aren't summering in the south of France.

In fact, according to the US DOT Bureau of Transportation Statistics, long-distance (50 miles+) recreational summer trips are brief! Roughly half are same-day trips. For multi-day trips, the average stay away is 2.1 nights. Which means, most people are, in fact, still in town!

The summer might present some volume or case management challenges for your practice, but don't let a self-fulfilling prophecy turn what could be a very productive summer into a drought.

2) Diversify Referral Sources

If a school district is your primary referral source, then—of course—your incoming leads will drop this season. They key for summer (and, in fact, year-long) survival is having diversified referral sources. Possible referral sources are limitless (see previous columns), but consider company HR departments, medical practices, or court systems. Remember, there are 50,000 people in your city. You can counsel about 50. Instead of thinking "How will I keep myself full?" Consider, instead, that you need to help people find you before you're overbooked.

3) Diversify Your Services

You think counseling is seasonal? Unless you run a Seasonal Affective Disorder clinic, not really. Here are some businesses that are really seasonal:

- Ice cream stands
- Lawn care companies
- Christmas shops

Or are they? Even these businesses can run yearlong.

First, the owners of your local ice cream stand might migrate to Florida in the winter, but people do eat ice cream all year. Also, that stand could churn out loaded French fries and hot cocoa in the winter (image a world where every November ice cream stands began selling loaded fries? That's a world I want to live in).

Second, the smart lawn care companies plow driveways in the winter—it's an ideal transition, lawn care to driveway care.

Third, is there really Christmas in July? Well, the biggest Christmas shop brand of its kind, "Christmas Tree Shops ®" is thriving year-round, and their new logo actually reads, "Christmas Tree Shops ® and That!"

Counseling isn't seasonal; anxiety, eating disorders, addictions, bipolar depression, schizophrenia, sleep disorders, relationship issues, grief, loneliness—there's nothing about the summer that reduces the incidence of these issues. However, maybe there are some services that you can only provide in the summer. For example, I once worked with a counselor who ran a group that would start with a run across town, and have group therapy after. She found people were more open, and more in-tune with themselves, after the run. Can't do that during a snowstorm!

4) Research and Development

When a business is busy, you're running just to keep up with the demands of your customers or clients. Slow times can be a blessing in disguise as they offer you the ability to review feedback and to improve your product or service in ways you didn't have the time for when business was booming.

Perhaps there's something about your practice you want to improve? Summer could be an ideal time to do just that.

5) Catch Your Breath

Running a business is no easy task. If your client load is lighter this season, maybe that's a good thing. Perhaps it's the perfect time for you to finally take a break. I hear the south of France is beautiful this time of year.

The threat of a summer slowdown can feel unnerving. Don't panic. With preparation, your practice can still be busy—even grow—during the summer months.

Lesson 21:
Weathering the Slow Winter Slump

A few months ago I wrote a column about the Summer Slump. Let me preface this month's column by saying that I realize most people have never heard of a "winter slump" in our field. In fact, for many mental health practices, winter is good for business. Short, dark days seem to carry with them client discontent and malaise. A study published in the *American Journal of Preventive Medicine* showed that, during the winter months, online searches increase for mental health issues including anxiety, OCD, bipolar disorder, eating disorders, depression, suicide, ADHD and even schizophrenia. Combine that with the fact that people don't have a whole lot else going on, and winter is just a good time for clients to work on their stuff in therapy. From December to February, practices have no trouble paying the rent.

But then, there was last year.

We're used to harsh winters in New England. We're used to that long wait for spring, and spying still-melting snow piles in June. But last year (with a record snowfall of 110 inches in Massachusetts) was one of the worst.

Emotionally, by midsummer most people have forgotten about the winter. This year, nobody's forgotten. In fact, I have more than a few clients who say they "have had it" and are searching for real-estate south of the Mason Dixon Line.

Financially, last winter, a lot of people took a hit. Over 8 feet of snow in one month resulted in roughly one billion dollars in lost profits and wages in

Massachusetts alone. Retailers and restaurants were hit hard, with sales reportedly falling about 50%. *When there's multiple blizzards and a states of emergency, businesses and hourly workers lose. And while some can make up for the lost revenue—for example, if you're an optician, people still need their eyes checked or if you're a tailor, people still need their suits fitted—others, such as counselors, can't make up for lost time (and subsequently, lost revenue). Nobody is doubling up on counseling sessions to compensate for the ones they missed. At my counseling practice, throughout January and February, we were closed almost as often as we were open.

Hence, what should have been some of our busiest months were what will be recorded as the leanest of the year.

Recently, even southern states have experienced the effects of harsh winters. In Atlanta, the winter of 2014 brought record ice storms, which resulted in our therapists camped out at the office, or stuck on the highway, for multiple days. The entire city came to a freezing halt—*twice!* We've had similar harsh winters in Virginia and Tennessee.

Will lightning strike again in 2016? Are we living in times of more extreme weather? I have no idea. But, I'd say it's best practice to establish an inclement weather plan with your clients. Here are three recommendations.

Talk with Your Clients in Advance:
Talk with your clients about the possibility of using telephone or videoconference sessions, in the event of a winter storm emergency. Do this in advance of an actual storm. Show your clients how such a session would be

conducted, and explain all the necessary disclosures about using technology for the delivery of mental health services. Note: the key-phrase here is "in advance." You've waited too long if there's already an impending storm, as you'll find yourself trying to chase clients down after they've already cancelled their sessions.

I know of one therapist who is making his inclement weather policy a requirement for new clients. Clients can opt for phone, video, or pay a no-show fee, but they can't cancel for the reason of weather. It sounds strict, and it is, but—financial motives aside—he's adamant about the importance of uninterrupted and consistent clinical services.

Call Your Insurance Companies & 3rd Party Payers:
Every year, more insurance companies are allowing for the provision of psychotherapy sessions over videoconference. Cigna, Anthem and United Healthcare, in various states, have even created their own dial-a-doc programs. Contact every insurance company, EAP, and other third party payer you're credentialed with to learn what they will allow as it relates to distance treatment. If they won't covered online services as a general rule, ask about an exception for inclement weather situations.

If All Else Fails, Consider Reducing Rates:
If your practice, like many, is predominantly funded by insurance companies, and if those payers won't cover phone or online therapy sessions, consider offering distance sessions to your clients at a reduced rate—or even a co-pay rate. Since you're offering a service that the insurance company won't cover,

you shouldn't be in violation of any contract terms (double check, of course).

This is a steep cut in hourly pay for sure, but perhaps it's better to

1. **Keep continuity of car**

2. **Earn some revenue, rather than nothing at all.**

Your clients will likely appreciate your willingness to do this, as well.

Let's all hope for a "winter bump" this year, not a "winter slump." Still, let's be prepared—just in case this winter brings another rough ride.

Lesson 22:
Hiring Employees V. Independent Contractors

Are you ready to bring on an additional counselor? Congrats! Your practice must be growing!

If you're like many, you're facing a tricky decision. This new clinician—will you be hiring him or her as an employee, or as an independent contractor? Practices have done it both ways, and there are pros and cons to each.

Independent Contractors and Taxes

As a hiring party, there are some benefits to hiring clinicians as independent contractors. For starters, independent contractors don't receive health insurance, which could save an employer thousands every year. Moreover, 7.65% of an *employee's* wages are required to be paid, by the employer, to the IRS in the form of "payroll tax" (there is also unemployment tax, and workers compensation).

Put into context, say you're paying a clinician $60 per session. You'll pay another $4.59 (7.65%) on the clinician's behalf to the IRS. In contrast, when a worker is an independent contractor (i.e., not an employee), the hiring party is not required to pay the 7.65% tax.

Does The Counselor Qualify as an Independent Contractor?

An important question is whether a clinician at your practice will meet the criteria of an independent contractor. This is sometimes difficult to determine. However, the IRS has adopted some common law principles to define what constitutes an independent contractor.

The primary issue is one of "employer control." That is, does the hiring party define how the clinician's work will be accomplished? If a hiring party does not have authority over how a clinician accomplishes his or her work—but simply gives an outline of the work to be done—independent contractor status may be an option. However, there are some additional common law issues, which include:

1. "Who has paid for materials, supplies and equipment? A contractor generally provides their own supplies and tools."

2. "What type of skill is required? A contractor generally brings a specialized skill set."

3. "Is there permanence in the job? A contractor often works project to project."

4. "Is the worker an integral part of the business? A contractor can often be replaced by another contractor."

5. "Does the hiring party control when the worker comes to work? A contractor generally makes his or her own hours."

6. "Does the worker receive a steady paycheck? A contractor often receives variable payments upon completion of projects or tasks."

7. "Is it the worker's only source of income? A contractor usually works for several parties."

Set up correctly, counselors are likely to qualify for independent contractor status. They often choose their own hours, work in multiple locations, and an argument can be made that the hiring party lacks control over "how" they perform their job, as it's primarily done in a private therapy office.

However, a practice needs to exercise caution—it's easy to start treating your contractors like employees. For example, contractors can't have business cards. They're their own entities, so having a business card with "Your Brand" on it would be contradictory. They probably shouldn't be listed as "staff" on your website.

Also, you should limit what materials you supply—intake documents, handouts, pens, computers, tissues: contractors should be bringing most of this stuff with them.

Finally, make sure that the workers buy into the fact that they're independent contractors, because any of them could file a case with the IRS stating that that he or she was actually an employee.

One Practice's Story

Like many small practices, we started by hiring our first clinicians as independent contractors. It seemed a lot easier at the time. Less paperwork. Fewer taxes. No requirement to provide health insurance (which we couldn't afford).

However, the more I had a clear vision for how I wanted my practice to run, the more the model of having independent contractors didn't seem to fit. While I wasn't in session with my clinicians directing their every word, we developed a pretty extensive operations and procedures manual. We also wrote a mission statement and a quality code. There were a growing number of areas where I wanted my clinicians to do things "the Thriveworks way." Moreover, we wanted the counselors to feel as though they were a part of what we were building. An independent contractor is a "hired gun," not a team member.

Also, because my staff was independent contractors, there were some simple things that I couldn't do. I couldn't give them business cards (see above). Indeed, every time we supplied a computer, a printer, printing paper, or anything else, our counselors became more and more like employees. Also, while in the beginning I saw that not offering health insurance was a necessity (as we had no money), as time went on I began to see how important such benefits were to my team—and I wanted to offer benefits.

Around April of our second year, I experienced a last straw moment. A counselor showed up in my office, choking back tears because she had been to her accountant to do her yearly taxes, and had learned that she owed thousands of dollars to the IRS. She said, "I didn't realize I was going to owe this much: I don't have it!" All those payroll taxes that I wasn't paying; my counselors needed to pony up at tax time—and some of them didn't plan well, and found themselves in serious financial trouble.

Within two weeks of this meeting I had converted every clinician to employee status, and with the exception of the occasional psychiatrist (who often prefer independent contractor status) we haven't hired a single contractor since. Every once in a while our COO will say—usually after a rogue clinician has defected from our operations manual in some way— "You know how much money we'd save if we converted our staff to independent contractors?" and I stop him right there. For us, having employees is the way to go.

Lesson 23:
Preventing the Painful Problem of Provider Turnover

At my practices, in the last year, two counselors submitted letters of resignation because they were tired of the daily commute and wanted to work closer to home, two others decided to work less and cut their hours by more than half, and another two resigned after deciding to migrate from the east coast to California (one had plans to join a commune and take up organic gardening). Even with over 50 clinicians on staff, losing even one counselor is difficult. But it's all too common.

Monitor the roster of a typical counseling practice and you'll see a pattern. Every year the lineup of therapists changes by about a third. When I talk with managers, there's a consensus that one of the most difficult parts of building a counseling practice that provides consistent quality care to clients is keeping their staff.

There's a well-known cultural trend that persons tend to "job hop" more now than in decades past. However—and I'm going to be brutally honest—when looking at turnover within medical professions, with the exception of positions like lower-end techs and CNAs, I don't see turnover in other licensed healthcare specialties like I do in counseling. My friends and colleagues who are opticians, chiropractors, or PCPs, when they hire a new doctor, that doc is on the team for 5-plus years, and a fair number stay on indefinitely.

There are a number of reasons counseling practices lose good counselors. Assuming you have a practice with plenty of client referrals, a positive culture, good pay, a great working environment, admin support, and lots of respect, here are three 3 tips I've found important for reducing provider turnover.

Create a Term Contract

When you bring on a new provider you invest resources into recruiting, credentialing, promoting, onboarding, and training. After this, you pay the clinician the lion's share of the revenue that comes into the practice. This is all well and good—it's the cost of having a practice staffed with excellent providers. The problem is, if that provider leaves 12 months later you might find that all the time, effort, money, and risk you've invested has left you with a net loss. Worse yet, you're scrambling to recruit and train a replacement to offer clinical care to clients.

Counseling practices, as a rule, get too many "false positives" when they hire. That is, persons are brought on board that a hiring manager believes are going to be good, long-term, team members, but who end up falling short in some way—*such as a premature departure.*

Today, my practices have a 3-year term contract for new providers. Assuming we meet our obligations under the contract, if a provider leaves in less than three years there's a financial consequence for the early departure. This has certainly increased our "false negatives," people who might have been good long-term team members but just couldn't bring themselves to sign up for a 3-year commitment. However, we're okay with that because we've reduced our false positives! On more than a few occasions a potential new team member will talk about how he or she plans to be in the community forever. After hearing about our 3-year term, the story changes to something like, *"Well, to be honest, my wife/husband is in a 1-year internship and we're not really sure what we're doing afterward."* The term contract weeds out persons who are likely to move, cut their hours, or get tired of the daily commute.

Develop Promotion & Growth Opportunities

Once upon a time I would hire clinicians and overpay them. My thinking—if I overpay and provide a great work experience they'll never want to leave. WRONG. Something really interesting happens when one has a full caseload of clients, is making good money, and his/her job is cushy (as cushy as possible, that is). One starts thinking, *"Well, I've been successful at this private practice thing, what's next for me? Should try something else? Maybe I should start teaching? Maybe I should move to California and take up organic farming!"*

I should have known better. People need to feel that their making progress to be happy, it's positive psychology 101. It doesn't matter how high you climb, once you reach the top you start looking left and right. The climb is important.

Today we have 12 levels of counselor rank ranging from "Assistant Clinician" to "Summa Clinician." It takes at a minimum of 7 years to reach the top, but typically much longer. Each rung is achieved when the clinician meets certain criteria including goals that are customized to match the provider's own professional ambitions. A team member always knows what level he/she is at, and what's required to get to the next. Of course, with each new level comes a financial benefit of some kind.

We're doing more with this program every year (and the more we do, the more meaningful it becomes). Now, when we introduce a clinician, we say, "This is Dr. Smith, a Senior-Associate Clinician at our Atlanta Office." The title also goes on the provider's business cards. Counselors fight it. A counselor will say "I don't need the title!" Then, we see him smile and quietly set the cards on the edge of his desk.

Hire Well

No contract in the world will make things good if you've made a bad hire. Spend time getting to know applicants. Make sure you know how they work, how they interact with clients, how they respond to challenges and conflict. Find out: how dedicated to being a FT outpatient therapist are they? Have they maintained a full caseload in an outpatient practice before? Why did they leave (check references)?

Are they likely to be working in the community for the next 5-20 years? Assuming you are a counselor, you're trained to see the best in people. When hiring, you need to take off your 'counselor hat' and put on your 'cynic hat.' In what ways might this relationship go south? Where are these providers' weaknesses? Be extremely selective. It's okay if you pass on a good therapist because you're not 100% convinced it will be a good fit. It's better to have false negatives than false positives.

Trailblazing

Generally speaking, counselors aren't comfortable with contracts. They aren't used to titles and rank. And they certainly aren't used to a rigorous screening process before being offered a position; that's okay. Follow the advice in this column and you will be trailblazing. It won't be easy! But in the end you should have a strong, dedicated, longstanding clinical team.

Lesson 24:
Creating Culture in Your Group Practice

The Impact of a Positive Office Culture

Tony Hsieh, the CEO of Zappos, is author of the bestselling book "Delivering Happiness." The book is a quasi-autobiographical account of Tony's entrepreneurial successes, including an Internet-based company "Link Exchange" that he sold to Microsoft for $265 million. Tony recounts that he decided to sell Link Exchange when the culture went downhill, and he no longer felt a connection with his employees.

In his book, Tony writes that Zappos, to keep the culture strong, only hires people they want to hang out with — and it seems to work! Today, Zappos culture is legendary. From impromptu zombie parades to "bald is beautiful" shave your head contests, Zappos seems a hybrid between fraternity, cult and family.

Culture in Group Counseling Practices

Today, the cultures of many group counseling practices struggle. Here are some common scenarios:

1. The counselors are independent contractors, work several other jobs, and have practices of their own on the side. As soon at their solo-practice caseloads fill, they'll quit your "gig."

2. Seasoned clinicians won't abide by anyone's rules but their own. Clinical notes are late, and in the wrong format. They aren't on board with company initiatives. In fact, they won't turn off a light or close a door behind them, because that's not their job.

3. The psychiatrist sees as many clients as possible, as quickly as possible, and then gets the heck out the office as soon as possible. He has never attended a staff meeting. Stay away from his parking space, and you won't have a problem.

4. The manager/owner is also a clinician with a caseload of her own. She is overworked, overstressed and struggles to juggle basic company operations. Building culture seems like an unaffordable luxury.

Culture is not a luxury — it's a necessity. Culture is the glue that holds a company together. Without it, morale and quality suffer, employee turnover increases, and recruiting new staff becomes more difficult.

Zappos purports that culture starts with hiring, and they're right. At my company, we hire talented, experienced staff. But we also spend a lot of time making sure a new clinician is a good culture fit. We hire those who will get along with the team, and who embody our mission of positive, empowering therapy.

However, unlike Zappos, we don't subscribe to the "we must want to hang out with you" philosophy (we've hired clinicians in their early 20s and in their mid 70s. They're not hanging out). Instead, I prefer Tina Fey's rule: "Don't hire anyone you wouldn't want to run into in the hallway at three in the morning."

Culture starts at hiring, but it doesn't end there. As manager, it's your job to cultivate positive company culture.

Things I Tried that Failed!

Company culture is a hot topic today, and if you read business books or magazines, you'll encounter scores of methods on how to promote a positive one. Here are two in vogue suggestions I tried … that flopped!

Transparent Finances

Some contend that to cultivate a strong culture, a company should share their finances with employees. That way, employees can rally with you when times are bad, and rejoice with you when times are good! In fact, if finances aren't transparent, you likely have a "control issue."

I tried this. I drew up reports and charts, and called meetings to explain company profits, losses, margins and payroll. Employees' resounding response: "This has nothing to do with me!"

"Of course it does!" I said, and pointed again to my spreadsheets, "See!?" In the end, I learned that my team doesn't care how much money the company makes (or doesn't), as long as they feel that they're well compensated for their role.

Unlimited PTO

Today, it's in vogue to offer employees unlimited PTO. The theory suggests that unlimited PTO promotes a culture of trust because, "What does it matter how many days employees take off as long as they get their work done?"

So, I tried it with my admin staff. Surprise! Some people used A LOT of PTO, while others felt cheated for coming to work while their counterparts were off. Morale didn't improve. Productivity didn't improve. It might seem obvious, but employees are more productive when they're, well, working. We have since switched back from "unlimited" to generous amounts of PTO, and our culture is better for it.

Things I Tried that Work!

To date, we have had no zombie parades, or "bald is beautiful" events. We don't have an office cat (allergies), and my idea of putting a 1980s arcade machine in the

conference room was vetoed. Still, we do a lot to build culture.

Respect and Gestures of Caring

At our company, more than half of our mission statement addresses our employees, and we mean every word. Here's an excerpt: "Thriveworks, at its core, is its team of people ... We work to engender great loyalty in the team members of Thriveworks and hope that we are successful in developing and maintaining their loyalty to the point that they elect to stay employed with us for life."

We truly care about our team. If someone has a problem, at work or otherwise, we try to help. We respect our employees, and value their contributions. We are honest. We strive to be generous. We are finally remembering to celebrate birthdays and employment anniversaries (and new babies). For a long time, I thought doing this was too much of a cliché. But we want to honor our employees at every opportunity, and they really seem to appreciate the acknowledgements.

Community

Counseling is an isolating profession. While you are with people all day in session, the focus is 100 percent on the clients. Hence, many counselors in private practice apply to work with us because they are looking for colleagues to connect with in-between sessions.

Mission

Mission affects culture. If your company leadership is serious about its mission, your team will get serious about it also. A company should always be able to answer the question: "Why are we doing what we're doing?" If your employees believe the company is truly dedicated to a valuable mission, you have the genesis of a strong culture.

Progress

People need to feel that they're making progress in their careers. With clinical staff, up until recently we would hire great counselors, pay them well, and help them to fill their caseloads. However, once their caseloads were full, there was little opportunity for progress. How demoralizing after two, three or five years to still be doing the same work, with the same title, without any path to something more?

In response, we developed something we have never seen before in the industry: 10 levels of Counselor Rank. Now, clinical staff, through tenure and excellent performance, can be promoted 10 times, from "Fellow," to "Senior," to "Master" clinician, and each level brings with it greater compensation, including perks ranging from paid education to paid vacations.

Your Practice, Your Culture

Creating culture isn't easy, and there's no one right way go about it. As you begin to build your company's culture, some things you try will work, and some things will likely flop. However, even when you miss the mark, your team will notice your efforts, and see that you care, and that is perhaps the most important culture-building ingredient.

301: Growing a Private Practice

Lesson 25:
Destiny: Should I Grow my Solo Practice into a Group?

Benjamin Franklin is known for his strict schedule. His personal notes show that he was asleep at 10pm, awake at 5am—and he spent most of his waking hours working, or reviewing his tasks.

Starting a counseling practice isn't a 40-hour a week job. Successful entrepreneurs either "Do the Franklin," or burn the midnight oil. Or both! This is because an aspiring counselor-entrepreneur must stay relevant with the practice of counseling while learning (and executing) the myriad aspects of running a business (e.g., enacting a business plan, managing finances, setting up an office, getting the word out, etc.).

After a year of hustle...

Once you've "done the Franklin," for about a year, you'll notice some changes. Your phone is ringing, and your caseload is filling! People will tell you that they've read your articles, or saw you on the news. New clients will tell you that they heard you speak, or watched a YouTube video of one of your talks. New clients will tell you that another client, to whom you provided great care and service, referred them!

If all goes well, at some point in year two your caseload will reach 35 sessions a week. At 35 sessions, you're with clients 26.25 hours a week. You spend 13.75 hours a week on clinical notes and managing your one-office company. You're working a comfortable 40-hours a week, and bringing home net earnings of six figures a year.

Your private practice is Thriving! And you have options...

1) Stay Small

While nothing needs to change, there are several options for your small practice to consider.

a. Hire administrative help.

Perhaps there are some tasks you wish to delegate: reception and scheduling, billing and bookkeeping, or general office upkeep. This can sometimes be done without reducing net profit.

If a counselor earns $65 per clinical hour, as long as an employee (a) costs less than $65 an hour, and (b) completes their tasks efficiently, an increase in the counselor's caseload could compensate for the administrative costs. This approach won't reduce the counselor's workweek, but will allow the counselor to trade administrative tasks for clinical work.

b. Raise your rates.

Your caseload is full, and you're even turning some clients away because you're too full to schedule them. You may have the luxury of raising your rates. This is supply and demand: There is limited supply of you, and there's overwhelming demand.

By raising rates, you will reduce demand—so finding a balance is important. Don't overdo it! Raise prices slowly, for new clients only. Or raise rates for your most desirable appointment times

(Note: If you accept insurance, you will need to provide services at your contracted rate. However, one can reserve premium times for the highest paying insurance companies, or block out some times for cash-only clients.).

2. Get Big

Perhaps, after years of counseling, you decide that spending the majority of your workweek in session with clients isn't for you. Or, you decide that you want to capitalize on your practice's extra client leads, without raising prices. A desirable option may be to bring on another counselor.

a. Bring on a counselor.

Bringing on a counselor to work in your practice is a big decision (and responsibility), as it involves much more than funneling surplus client leads. For many, to execute this well, one will need to transition from full-time clinician to full-time manager. Counselors expect a lot in exchange for a split of their session fees. Traditionally, a practice will provide:

- **Office Space:** Two counselors sharing one office won't work. Even if one counselor is part-time, there will be scheduling conflicts during the most desirable session hours.
- **Ample Leads:** The attrition rate for clients is around 8 sessions. Therefore, a counselor needs 4.5 new clients a week to build and maintain a full caseload.
- **Billing / Credentialing:** Reliable, timely medical billing is crucial. Also, even if a counselor is previously paneled with insurance companies, additional credentialing is necessary to allow him/her to bill through your practice.

- **Reception and Scheduling:** Counselors expect a high level of front-end administrative help. Printing forms, ordering supplies, and other office tasks are often the responsibility of the practice.

- **Insurance:** To recruit great counselors, consider a 50% split on health insurance, and 100% of professional liability insurance.

- **Community:** Counselors often wish to be part of a community, and even seasoned clinicians expect the practice to offer some clinical supervision.

Changing from a solo-practice to a group practice isn't a small change; it's the start of a new business (with more risk, and more reward). Get ready for a new journey, and to again "Do the Franklin!"

A Solo or Group Practice—which is right for you?

Lesson 26:
Oxymoron: Staying Small to Grow Big

I'm on the phone with a gentleman (let's call him Dan) who owns a counseling practice in the Midwest.

He starts the conversation by describing some of his operational problems: "Anthony, recently some of my best counselors have left the practice. I have issues with notes not being completed. Our culture and team morale are low. We have lots of new clients' schedule, but most don't come back. And I'm losing money…" After hearing his pains, I ask him about the size of his operation.

He says, "It's a big practice! I have three locations, 18 therapy rooms, 20 counselors…" I then say, "Dan, the number of employees and locations you have are only 'vanity metrics.' How many clients is your company helping a week? That is— how many sessions in total?"
Dan says, "About 165."
"Okay, that means your practice is the equivalent of 5 full-timers."
"…Yeah. I guess so."

I see this mistake all the time. Practice owners pay attention to "vanity metrics," but they're blind to the figures that matter. Dan and I spent the next 30 minutes exploring how the challenges he's experiencing in his practice are directly related to his supernumerary size.

This month, as a nod to keeping things small, I'm going to keep my advice short and concise. Below are two areas were practices tend to grow too big, too quickly.

1. Counselors: Hire as few as you need to serve your incoming clients.

- Your practice's success is greatly dependent on the counselors you hire, and how you manage and train those counselors. Hire excellent clinicians who can be coached to exceed their own expectations.

- Employing fewer clinicians means you can train your team well, manage well and keep administrative costs down.

- As you cultivate high performance, you'll have the ability to pay your counselors higher wages. This increases morale and reduces turnover.

- Part-timers tend to be less dedicated to the company. They're also more difficult to coordinate with for meetings, performance management and ongoing training.

2. Space: Keep your space as small as possible.

- More office space is an expensive consequence of success, not a symbol of success.

- A single therapy room can often accommodate in excess of 40 sessions a week.

- If space is getting tight, consider expanding hours into Saturdays (and Sundays?) before you expand your office.

- Maximizing office space is easiest when you have fewer counselors that are working more (and more consistent) hours (see above).

- Opening a second location is often about vanity. When additional space is needed, first try to expand at your current location.

Regarding Dan, even at 165 sessions a week, his practice is a clinical liability that's losing money. However, if he can right-size his operation, he'll be able to improve patient care, monitor notes and billings, build a stronger team culture, increase pay to his staff and even pay himself for his labor.

Which business would you rather run — one with three locations and 20 employees, or one with one location and five employees that's helping the same number of clients?

Lesson 27:
Start Here: Marketing and Promoting Your Counseling Practice

Promotion is an art and a science, a gamble, and a moving target. Few things about building a practice perplex people more than promoting it. In this column, I dispense with style and cram as much advice as I can into 1000 words. Enjoy!

Be a Disciplined Advertiser

Never take a "big blind swing" with advertising. Invest only where you can test advertising effectiveness without blowing your budget. You never want to be in a place where you "need" any one advertising campaign to work. Most advertising won't produce a positive ROI (return on investment). That said, once you find an outlet does produce a positive ROI consider an increase in your investment with that outlet.

Ad Salespeople Are Not Your Friends

Logic would suggest that people who sell ads want you to be successful so that they can foster a long term, mutually beneficial, relationship. In my experience, persons selling ads are looking for a quick sale. Be very careful. Remember that you're the one spending money and you have power when negotiating for exposure. Some media (such as magazine and radio) are desperate for advertisers—so negotiate hard on price and terms.

Offline Promotion and Marketing

Professional Networking

For those who do it well, nothing compares with the results one can receive through good "old fashioned" networking. However, networking isn't easy, and while you're not spending many dollars, you're spending lots of valuable time. The president of Business Networking International recommends a minimum of 6.5 hours a week for networking success. If you're not interested in putting in those hours, at least initially, networking might not be right for you.

Unlike advertising, networking isn't about exposure—it's about relationships. Here's how it works. Say you want to grow a child therapy practice. You might visit a pediatrician's office, introduce yourself and offer to bring breakfast the next week. Then, at breakfast, you give a 3-minute presentation and shake some hands. Later, you drop off some literature. Then, you host a lunch. Then, you drop off more information. Over many visits a relationship builds. Finally, when they need to refer a child to counseling, guess who they think of?

Print

Print advertising is usually overpriced, and often too expensive for small businesses. To test the waters in print, you'll want to advertise for 6-months in a monthly publication, or 6-weeks in a weekly publication. Usually, advertisers lose money and additional tweaking and testing is needed.

Direct Mail

People today open their mail over the garbage. If you decide to try direct mail, focus on potential referral sources, not potential clients. Mail churches if you offer Christian counseling. Make an offer they can't refuse in your literature. Consider calling everyone in advance to let them know your mail is coming.

Radio/Television

One challenge with radio and TV is that the audience range is very wide. Generally, people want to find a counselor within a few miles of their home or work, and a small station might have a 50-mile radius. Hence, most people watching or hearing your ad aren't even in your market. Also, before you spend a penny listen to *"Advertising in America: What Works, What Doesn't, and Why"* By Roy H. Williams.

Billboards

Every billboard is a one-second reminder. Billboards work best when persons already have a perceived need and exposure to your brand (i.e., I'm hungry. I see Big Mac.). There's little time when driving 45 miles an hour to learn about your counseling services. You might see thousands of cars pass by, but you're unlikely to get thousands of calls.

Public Relations (PR)

Advertising is *paid* for, PR is *prayed* for. Getting a mention in the paper, on the evening news, or anywhere in media can help to build you brand. "As featured in" mentions help potential clients see that you're a step above your competition. That said, don't expect a spike of calls after a media event. Last month, my company was featured on The Doctors. The phones didn't ring any faster (but the logo sure looks good in the "as featured in" section of our website).

Online Promotion and Marketing

There are many important things that go into good online promotion. I can only mention a few here.

Google / Bing / Yelp Ads

Google and Bing sell ads by auction, and prices can climb fast. To keep them under control, be conservative with

1. Your daily budget

2. Ad radius

3. The words you bid for.

Regarding the later, if you bid for "depression" you're bidding against every pharma company that's promoting their antidepressant. Instead, bid for the more specific term "depression counseling." Yelp might be more expensive than Google and Bing, but Yelp is also at the very bottom of the sales funnel; meaning that people go to Yelp for one reason—to buy.

Backlinks

To rank on the first page of Google or Bing, one important thing to consider is backlinks.

Backlinks continue to be an important factor that Google/Bing use identify one site's value relative to another. Earn quality backlinks from reputable sources: From a non-profit you've donated time to, from a school you gave a scholarship to, from your local news station's website after they've quoted you, or from a dentist in town after you wrote an article for her website titled, "3 Tips for Overcoming Your Fear of Seeing the Dentist."

Reviews

Online reviews aren't just for restaurants. Potential counseling clients are reading online reviews to determine what counselor could be a good fit. Check the *ACA Code of Ethics* and the review guidelines of Facebook, Yelp, and Google, and then consider what you can do within the rules to achieve the coveted 5-stars your practice deserves.

A Moving Target

Promotion is a moving target. What works in some areas won't work in others; and what works today might not work tomorrow. Remember, it wasn't long ago that a half-page ad in the yellow pages was a must. Lastly, trust your gut. My experience might not be yours. Prove me wrong, and tell me when you do on Twitter @Thriveworks. And good luck!

Lesson 28:
40 More Strategies for Building a Full Caseload

I'm often asked how to build a full caseload, frequently with an implicit skepticism, as in, "In this economic climate, it's impossible!" Yet, some practices are still so full they have waiting lists. What follows are 40-plus quick tips for filling your client roster. They're a mile wide and an inch deep, but the ideas are a good jumping off point.

Professional networking

1. When someone asks what you do, don't answer, "I'm a counselor." Instead, focus on your target audience and outcomes. Say, "I help struggling parents build great relationships with their kids" or "I help ordinary people find extraordinary careers." The latter will generate more interest, which will help word spread about your practice.

2. Join your local chamber of commerce and Rotary Club.

3. Volunteer to speak for free to any group of five or more people on a counseling topic of interest to them. Speak to older men about depression. Speak to teachers about compassion fatigue. This should be valuable information, not a sales pitch!

4. Hand out business cards when you meet persons interested in what you do. Give out two at a time, and ask others to help spread the word.

5. Let your clients know that word-of-mouth referrals are welcomed and appreciated and that you're accepting new clients.

6. Visit, in person, every massage therapy business in your area. Spend time to find out what value you can offer them. If indicated, start a cross-marketing campaign!

- Do it again, with chiropractors.

- Do it again, with acupuncturists.

- Do it again, with physicians in private practice.

- Do it again, with speech pathologists, physical therapists and others.

Public relations

7. Locate "media calendars" for every local publication in your area. Identify upcoming articles for which you could contribute relevant insights. Contact the publications' editors and writers about contributing.

8. Contact the editors of local print or online publications. Offer to write a column or submit an article (at no charge)

9. Learn to write useful press releases. Syndicate them using PRWeb (an online distributor of press releases) for $200 each.

10. Write useful and insightful articles on counseling or life topics. Publish or disburse these articles anywhere you can.

11. Respond constructively to every positive or negative comment anyone makes about anything you say or write

12. Get media training to develop skills for handling difficult interviews by newspaper, radio and TV reporters.

Customer experience

13. Make sure that your telephone is answered every time it rings. Hire an answering service to take messages when you are in session or otherwise unavailable.

14. Remind clients of upcoming appointments.

    a) Schedule follow-up appointments at the end of every session.

15. Tell clients you expect them to happily pay your session fee if they no-show or cancel late (also let them know you will waive this in the event of a death or hospitalization).

16. Clean your office space or hire a cleaning service weekly.

17. Spend as much money as necessary to make your office look professional and feel comfortable. In addition (as discussed earlier), consider providing your clients:

    - Coffee, tea, water, soda and candy
    - Free Wi-Fi in your waiting room
    - The use of iPads in your waiting room
    - More than a dozen magazine subscriptions
    - A universal charger to recharge their cell phones
    - Lots of instructional signs (oversignage reduces customer anxiety)

18. Find ways to "wow," surprise and delight your clients.

19. Remember that a client is also a valued customer

20. Recruit persons to evaluate your brochures, business cards, website, office space and everything else to tell you what can be improved. Make those changes!

Clinical services

21. Identify your unique value proposition (UVP). Why should people choose you? Highlight one major value (for example, Buddhist approach to care, counseling in Japanese, walk-in appointments, interns providing counseling at cheaper prices, etc.)

22. Start sessions on time — or early. Also end sessions on time.

23. Expand your availability to accommodate clients' busy schedules.

24. Provide follow-up calls to clients after their first session or after particularly difficult sessions.

25. Provide a "getting started" guide with useful orientation materials to new clients.

26. Don't be afraid to see clients' multiple times per week if necessary.

27. Get on every major insurance panel in your area.

28. Coordinate care with your clients' other care providers.

29. Be at top form and deliver value in every counseling session, especially the first session (when many counselors just get a bunch of background information from the client).

    a) Self-care is a must to provide excellent care consistently!

30. Become a master at developing rapport.

31. Solicit client feedback on your performance (and client satisfaction).

32. Never stop learning or improving as a clinician.

Marketing and advertising

33. While growing your practice, spend 7 to 10 percent of your gross revenue on marketing endeavors

34. Build a website that is full of useful information (not sales pitches).

35. Get listed on Google Places, Yelp, Citysearch, Insider Pages, DMOZ and other quality online directories.

36. Join Twitter. Interact with and provide value to other users.

37. Create a Facebook business page. Post quality content on a regular basis (either your articles or others' articles). Tell people about the page.

38. Create a monthly e-mail newsletter that provides quality content people will want to read. Use a service such as Constant Contact or Mail Chimp to syndicate the newsletter.

39. Don't spam.

40. Buy advertising, and measure your return on investment (ROI).

   - Buy print ads in a local publication. Negotiate fiercely on price. Advertise for a minimum of six months in a monthly publication or eight weeks in a weekly publication.

   - Buy radio advertising at the smallest possible radio station.

   - Try online advertising via Google, Bing/Yahoo or Facebook.

Character and integrity

41. Be honest, genuine and generous to your clients, colleagues, employees and competitors.

42. Settle disputes with clients and potential clients quickly, even if they are in the wrong.

43. Don't blame the economy, the industry or your clients if your caseload is not full. Look in the mirror and say, "The buck stops here. How can I improve on what I'm doing?"

Lesson 29:
Six Places Counselors Should Spend Money to Make Money

For many of us, finding success in private counseling practice involves working with a shoestring budget, and making up for our lack of capital with a lot of sweat equity. While this approach works, there are some areas where under-spending can hurt your practice in the long run.

Below, I list six places where counselors should to spend money to make money:

1. Your Office Building

Too many counseling practices reside in run down, drab Class C buildings. Counseling offices should be bright, happy, inspiring places. Instead of finding the cheapest space, locate your practice in the nicest building you can find. While the cost will be more, it shouldn't make that big of a difference to your bottom line (counseling spaces are small — a six-office suite can be less than 2,000 square feet).

Your Class A space will help you recruit a good team, and will give a positive brand impression — this can lead to more satisfied clients, and more referrals. Also, studies show that the better a business' location, the less money that business will need to spend on advertising. Speaking of advertising.

2. Advertising

I receive a lot of calls from counselors who are struggling to build a caseload.

More often than not, these counselors are spending near to nothing on advertising. When asked why, they always mention the cost — advertising is expensive (and a professor in grad school told them that if they were good counselors, they wouldn't need to advertise).

While advertising is expensive, it's also expensive to pay rent in a space that isn't doing any business, and it's expensive to sit in that office every day with unbilled hours. It costs money to advertise and it costs money *not* to advertise.

Therefore, while you shouldn't run out and drop 10 grand on NPR sponsorships that might not move the needle, you should be investing in advertising. Invest smart. Test whether your advertising dollars are working with small amounts. When you've found a channel that produces a positive ROI, double your spend.

3. Anything to Do with Client Experience

As a service business, you build brand loyalty by surprising and delighting your clients. It goes without saying that the counseling at your practice needs to be excellent. But don't stop there.

Consider what else you can do to improve the client experience. The possibilities here are vast. For example, what would happen if you mailed every client you've ever had a copy of your favorite self-improvement book along with a hand written note? This would cost money for sure, but how many clients would be delighted by the gesture? And how many would be more likely to mention you next time someone asked them where they could find a good counselor?

4. Medical Billing

Medical billing is the lifeblood of your practice. If you don't get the monies you're owed from third-party payers, you're dead. So why do so many practices go without a reputable medical billing staff, or billing company?

Too many practices trust their billing to persons who lack the necessary experience, aptitude or who are otherwise not up for the task. Also, too many practices neglect checking client benefits and getting pre-authorizations because "it takes too long." Good billing processes cost time and money, but the cost of not getting paid for your services is much higher.

5. Your Clinical Staff

In the early years of my practice, I lost some good counselors because I underpaid. Or, rather, I "mediocre paid." Excellent clinicians have employment options, and they demand excellent compensation.

Having good clinician retention is crucial for the health of your practice. Losing clinicians can seriously damage your brand (that is, your company's relationships with clients), and the costs of recruiting, credentialing and filling a new clinician's caseload can be daunting. I changed my compensation philosophy early on and today clinician compensation is a strength when recruiting new team members (in addition to good pay, we offer health, dental, life, disability and liability insurance, and a 401K). Don't lose your best clinicians to the competition — pay your team well!

6. Giving Back

I'm not including this tip to sound generous. At my practice, I've found that when it comes to giving back to the community, it's hard to give more than we get in return. Every time we do something charitable we receive good press, we benefit from increased team morale, gain a deeper a sense of purpose, and we get some darn good karma (if you're into that sort of thing).

Counselors are already very generous, so a word of warning: Give back when you can. As Bono says, "give until it hurts," but don't give until you're in the hospital.

The six tips above are low hanging fruit — they're low risk and you'll notice the value almost immediately. No doubt, there are many other ways you can invest in your practice.

Lesson 30:
Warning: Counselors Top 10 Marketing Mistakes

We all make mistakes. Below are the top 10 marketing mistakes that are commonly made by mental health professionals.

10) Taking a Big, Blind Swing

Too often, novice advertisers overspend on ineffective advertising. I've seen this happen time and time again: A counselor takes a $9000 dollar gamble on an event sponsorship, television ad, or print ad and receives zero return. After betting heavy and losing, the counselor no longer has the courage (or capital) to advertise again, anywhere.

Advertising isn't about taking big, blind swings. It's about testing what works with amounts that won't break the bank, and increasing budgets in mediums that prove to provide a financial return. This leads us to mistake #9…

9) Not Tracking Where Referrals Come From

According to legend, Henry Ford once mentioned to an associate, "Only half of my advertising is working." When the associate asked why he doesn't quit the wasteful half, Ford answered, "The problem is I don't know *which* half!"

Perhaps unlike 1910, today there are many ways to track the effectiveness of a marketing campaign. From unique phone numbers, to website analytics, to simply asking people who call for an appointment, "*Where did you hear about us?*" counselors should be able to determine how potential clients learn about their practices.

Pop quiz: When someone calls your practice, do you know how he or she found you? If they were referred, do you know *exactly who referred?* If they found you online, do you know *where online?* Did they get your phone number from your website, or your directory listing on Theravive? Did they find you on Bing or Google? What keyword were they searching? Did they find you in the paid or organic listings?

All this information is available if you take the time to track, ask, and look.

8) Private Social Media Accounts Are Awful

According to a WSJ study, 2 in 5 employers now search Facebook and Twitter to screen potential candidates [ii]. In the same way, what counselors say online can and will be read by their clients, potential clients, and referral sources.

While many counselors have a professional LinkedIn profile, personal accounts often go unconsidered. To this effect, I've seen counselors' 'personal', but very public, Facebook accounts show pictures of them clubbing, complaining about their work as *"another day with the crazies!"*, and I've seen more political rants than I'd care to count.

I am not saying that everything you do online needs to be work related, or even that you need your privacy settings on high. Just remember: You are your brand, and anything you say or do can and will be used to judge whether someone wants to refer to you, or be counseled by you.

7) Bad Headshot

While often overlooked, the headshot is extremely important for counselors. This is what potential clients see before they meet you in person. Not surprisingly, the "Meet the Counselors" or "About us" page is typically one of the highest trafficked pages on a counseling center's website. In addition, many advertising opportunities for counselors—such as Theravive and GoodTherapyOrg—offer exclusively a bio and headshot!

Despite this, many counselors' headshots are worse than grade school or driver's license photos. They're too often from the 1980s, too informal (think selfie), or overly formal (think church bulletin or military).

> *"If you're guilty of having a bad headshot, schedule an hour with a professional photographer. We could all benefit from a little Photoshop here and there, am I right?"*

6) Technical Bio

Too many bios start like this, "*Dave is a Licensed Alcohol and Drug Abuse Counselor in the state of Delaware.*" A much better way to begin is this, "*Dave works with individuals struggling with addictions, and he helps them to find sobriety and healing.*"

There is a place to mention qualifications, but 99% of clients don't care that you're a Certified Imago Therapist; they want to know if you can help fix their marriage. Drop the technical jargon, or at least move it toward the bottom.

5) SPAMing

If you send out an email newsletter, and you should, make sure that the people you're sending it to want to receive it. Sending your newsletter to every email address you get your hands on (or buy) won't increase business; it will, however, increase the number of people who tag you for spam. Soon, you won't know who your real audience is, and you won't be able to reach them anyway because Gmail will filter all your messages instantly into the spam folder.

4) Guest Blogging

Guest blogging is the practice of contributing an article on a website that isn't your own (i.e., as a "guest"). Guest blogs typically contain a link back to your website, and the practice of writing guest blogs has been an effective marketing strategy for years.

The problem with guest blogging is that, over time, the practice has been abused and many "guest posts" are written simply to "get a link." In response, Matt Cutts, Google's head of web spam, just published *"The Decay and Fall of Guest Blogging for SEO."* He's giving fair warning to anyone guest blogging for the purposes of SEO, so beware!

3) Bad Website

You mail out flyers, hand out business cards, and even pay for ads that lead people to your website. There's just one problem; when someone visits to your website they find a mess of bad stock photos and typographical errors.

This is an epidemic! Just this week, a woman reached out to me wanting to sell her practice. The headline on her website read: *"Counseling for individuals, couples, and Families"* (note both the caps issues and misspelling).

> *"If you're going to have a practice in 2014 (or 2008), you need to have a well-designed, well written, professional website."*

2) Dingy Office

Marketing doesn't end after the first appointment is scheduled. Your office is an important part of retaining clients, and encouraging referrals. An old adage says that you can tell whether a business cares about its customers by how nice the bathrooms are. How are your bathrooms? How are your waiting rooms?

1) No Advertising at All

I've been saying this one for years—and yet it's still the #1 marketing mistake. When counselors tell me that they don't have enough clients, my first question is what they're currently doing to promote their practice. Most aren't doing any advertising at all. For the vast majority of companies, advertising is an ongoing part of running a successful business.

Everything is Marketing

Marketing is the process of communicating the value of a product or service. While advertising is a form of marketing, there are others. Answering the phone is good marketing. Having intake documents that aren't a copy of a copy (of a copy) from 1983 is good marketing. Making your clients comfortable is good marketing. Even providing clients excellent therapy is good marketing.

Lesson 31:
Marketing a Cash Pay Practice: The Do's and Don'ts

Counselors have run cash practices since the beginning of psychoanalysis. Today, however, a wave of change is occurring wherein clients are, more than ever, demanding that their counselors accept health insurance. There are many reasons for this, but consider these three points:

1. In tough economic times, clients have less discretionary cash.
2. Mental health parity means that counseling is almost always a covered health care benefit.
3. As counseling has established itself as an important medical service, clients now see their counselors in the same light as their family physicians (who have always accepted insurance).

Although these changes have been going on for years, a tipping point has taken place. Today's clients aren't sheepishly asking, "Will you accept my insurance?" They're demanding it!

Private Pay Practice?

Some counselors are in such high demand that they will never need to accept insurance. If you've reached this status, congratulations! For the rest of us, however, not accepting health insurance means a significant percentage of potential new clients will simply schedule with the counselor down the block (and these days, there are a lot of therapists from which to choose).

One solution is to get credentialed with insurance companies and bill third-party payers for your services. An alternative solution is to remain private pay and work hard at creating an extraordinary service for which clients willingly pay out of pocket. Both options are good ones.

Unfortunately, some private-pay counselors are using questionable methods to convince clients to pay out of pocket for care. Two methods are addressed below.

Method One: The Superbill

A superbill is a receipt for services that contains the basic information requested by insurance companies (generally from the provider) before payment is rendered. Private-pay counselors can require clients to pay up front for services and then issue clients a superbill receipt. Although there is nothing unethical about this, the way superbills are presented to clients can be misleading. What follows are two quotations (taken from counselor websites) that exemplify how the superbill is often explained to clients:

> "I will give you a 'Super-bill' fee statement for you to submit directly to your insurance company for reimbursement. I will work with you as you work with your insurance company to receive maximum benefits."

> "[Name Removed] Counseling, LLC will provide you with a 'super bill' for each date of service. This 'super bill' will provide all the information your insurance company requires in order to reimburse you."

Optimism and Responsibility

The preceding quotations are problematic in their optimism. In fact, an argument can be made that they contain a "lie of omission," which is that, for many clients, superbills are ineffective for obtaining reimbursement. It is always the client's responsibility to check his or her benefits. However, if counselors oversell the superbill, clients will feel burned when they realize the superbill wasn't so "super" after all.

Here are three reasons why the statements are too optimistic:

1) Insurance rarely pays a counselor's full fee. Providers might suggest that their superbills will facilitate insurance to pay their full fee. This almost never happens. A counselor's full fee is usually double what insurance companies consider their "customary rate." For instance, although a typical counseling fee might be $140, the customary insurance rate is about $75 ($55 after the client's copay). Insurance plans, even those with out-of-network benefits, rarely pay above their customary rate.

2) Out-of-network benefits often cover only a percentage of the customary rate. This is a type of "penalty" clients endure for selecting a provider out of their network. For example, an insurance company might pay 80 percent of its customary rate of $75. That's $60 (less the copay) reimbursed after the client has paid $140 to the counselor.

In addition, some insurance companies have deductibles for out-of-network services that differ from the in-network deductible. Hence, even if clients have out-of-network benefits on their policies and have met their deductibles for in-network benefits, they may have not met their out-of-network deductibles, meaning they might not receive any reimbursement.

3) Many clients don't have out-of-network benefits. As health care costs increase, many individuals are opting for HMO (health maintenance organization) plans over PPO (preferred provider organization) plans. Generally, this means out-of-network benefits are nonexistent. In these instances, the client will receive no reimbursement after seeing a counselor.

Truthfulness and Transparency

A truly transparent statement regarding a superbill's efficacy would sound like this:

"Although we don't accept insurance, we are happy to provide you with a superbill. Some clients will receive a portion of counseling fees reimbursed to them from their insurance companies. Many clients will not receive any reimbursement. Being reimbursed our full fee is extremely rare."

Method Two: Promoting Fear

Some counselors who do not want to accept insurance attempt to persuade clients to pay for counseling out of pocket by using fear. Consider the real examples that follow, which are similar to versions posted on many counselors' websites:

"For your protection and confidentiality I recommend that, if possible, you pay for your counseling without using insurance. Insurance companies require me to disclose highly personal information about you. The confidentiality and privacy of this information cannot be guaranteed. They also often restrict the number of sessions they will authorize, even if you and I feel you still need help."

"Please be aware that if you choose to submit a superbill to your insurance company, your private medical information will be released. This may impact your future insurance coverage, rates and reimbursement."

"To get therapy paid for by your medical insurance of any kind, you will have to be diagnosed with a mental 'disorder' of some kind. That will be in the computer database, available to insurance companies and, possibly, to future employers (and to the press if you run for president)."

In summary, the messages some counselors use to scare clients include:

- Your "permanent record" will show that you are psychologically unbalanced!
- Your premiums will skyrocket!
- You might become uninsurable!
- Don't use the insurance benefits that you're paying for — it's too dangerous!

George Ohlschlager, who has written extensively on counseling ethics, describes the issue as "an overblown fear." He notes he has not encountered a single firsthand (or verifiable real-world) example of a person suffering damages after using health insurance to pay for mental health services. Although conceding that "outlandish things are possible," he describes the aforementioned fears as "issues of anxiety to be talked about in therapy," not reasons to avoid using health insurance.

In contrast, a colleague and friend who had seen a psychiatrist for roughly three years for substance abuse and depression was later denied life insurance by the same company paying for his mental health services. It is plausible that the two are related.

Still, a question ensues: What kind of health care provider dissuades patients from using their insurance? The answer: A provider who doesn't want to accept insurance.

Here's a truthful disclosure counselors can use to inform clients about health insurance risks:

> *"Millions of people have seen counselors and used their insurance to pay for services. The vast majority has noticed no change in their personal insurability, or health insurance premiums, as a result. However, such an occurrence is possible. My concern for your health insurance premiums has very little to do with my decision not to accept your health insurance."*

Private-pay and Insurance-pay Counselors

Running a private-pay practice has its benefits. There is less paperwork, and the provider gets to set his or her own rates of service. With a good sliding fee scale and a strong reputation in one's community, building a private-pay practice is achievable — especially if you only desire a part-time caseload.

Alternatively, getting credentialed with insurance companies is also a good option. Family doctors, chiropractors and even dentists have accepted insurance for years. There are many companies (of which Thriveworks, my company, is just one) that can help you to get on insurance panels, and medical billing can be outsourced so that you can remain focused on your passion — seeing clients.

Whichever route you choose, be open and honest with clients about why your practice accepts (or doesn't accept) particular payment methods.

Lesson 32:

Spread the Word: If You Really Hate Networking, Try Colliding

Introverts and extroverts misunderstand each other. They're oil and water. They can be downright derisive to one another. The extrovert sees the introvert as frigid and snotty; the introvert sees the extrovert as loud, pushy, and off-pushing.

It's a paradox that for all the time we counselors spend communicating with persons in session, many of us are by nature introspective and introverted (and sometimes even reclusive) individuals. This serves us well as counselors—counseling is in fact isolating work—but our introverted dispositions can handicap us as promoters of our private practices. Introverts and extroverts misunderstand each other. They're oil and water. They can be downright derisive to one another. The extrovert sees the introvert as frigid and snotty; the introvert sees the extrovert as loud, pushy, and off-putting.

When it comes to self-promotion, extroverts have the clear upper hand. An extrovert will think nothing about "asking for business" or "getting the word out" about his/her clinical abilities—such activities are second nature. To the introvert, however, such actions are accompanied by much stress and words like "advertising," "marketing," and "business networking" evoke images of neon billboards, injury lawyer commercials, and used car salesmen (checkered polyester sports coat and all).

The Collision Re-frame

If you're an introvert (like me), and you're going to compete in the marketplace with the extroverts, you'll n eed a reframe to help you. From now on, instead of using the term "networking," I propose we use the term "colliding," and approach our practice differently. Whereas networking often includes a clear self-promotional bias, colliding effectively removes this bias. Additionally, don't bother focusing on your "elevator pitch," your "unique value proposition," or trying to monetize a return on your investment (ROI) of time spent interacting with new people. Instead, you're just meeting people, to see where it goes: to see if a collision evolves into a connection.

In order for someone to know about you and your practice, he or she will need to collide with you in some way. Many collisions will be small ones, and not much will come of them—the average handshake and hello. However, every once in a while a collision will be powerful. For example, collide with enough people and eventually you'll connect with someone who might be the perfect person to hire at your practice. Or, collide with enough persons and eventually you might encounter someone who works at a doctor's office— one that's desperately seeking a new referral source for mental health counseling.

> *"A single collision can change the trajectory of your practice—or for that matter, your life. In fact, this has probably already happened."*

Have you ever looked back on a relationship and thought, "Had I not introduced myself, or bothered to show up at that party, or made that scary phone call, I would have never met him/her!"? We all have. Now, if you're one who avoids new connections, here's a depressing thought. Think (just for a minute, then let it go) of how many powerful connections you've missed by not introducing yourself, not showing up, or not making that scary phone call (i.e., by not colliding)?

Bringing it back to business (e.g., private practice), a successful entrepreneur who sold his company for tens of millions of dollars taught me the motto: "Every day that you don't reach outside the four walls of your office is a day your business doesn't grow." Here are some recommendations to get you outside your four walls.

Increase your Collisions

If you're like most of us introverts, you need to get your number of collisions up (and sorry, your clients don't count). The more collisions you have, the more success you're going to have growing your practice.

Consider these two questions:

1. How can I increase my collisions?
2. How can I collide with new or different types of persons?

Also, to keep on track, let's apply the S.M.A.R.T. method:

*   Specific/Measurable: I will collide with 3 new people a day (21 per week)
*   Attainable: I will go to some event or public place two nights a week and interact with persons I would normally shy away from
*   Realistic: I will expect most collisions to be small ones, and for little to come from them (that's okay)
*   Timely: I will begin tonight

Collisions in Marketing and Advertising

In the paragraphs above we reframed the process of business "networking" as "colliding." However, the same principle can be applied to marketing and advertising.

Instead of looking at advertising as "pitching" your service, think of it as facilitating collisions with your business. Every time someone reads a blog article by you he/she is colliding with your practice. Every time someone sees your logo in a newspaper ad, or hears your practice's name on the radio, is a collision with your brand.

Lesson 33:
Warning: Be Different or Die!

Some companies, through advertising alone, convince us to buy their brand of product over a competitor's. It's why consumers choose Advil® instead a generic painkiller. It's why we grab a box with Tony the Tiger® instead of a bag of 'Sugary Flakes.' It's why we feel safer buying Scott® grass seed when we could buy seed with a less familiar name. We're so influenced by branding that we'll pay a premium for these items even when the generics are the exact same product.

Did you know that there was a time when paperclip companies would advertise their brand of paperclips? It worked, and people would pay more for the "brand name" clips. However, when everything is the same, eventually consumers will no longer be swayed by brand. The companies above notwithstanding, as a savvy marketplace realizes there's nothing special about a branded painkiller, cereal, or grass seed, the brand name means less and less…and eventually, nothing. In the end, everything becomes a commodity.

Counseling as a Commodity

With the exception of a few isolated areas, the United States has an abundance of therapists. Type almost any zip code into Psychology Today and you'll find page-after-page of counselors paying $30 a month. So how do you survive, or even champion a huge success, when the market is flooded with people selling the same product or service?

Two common solutions are:

1. Advertise like crazy
2. Cut prices.

Let me explain why neither of these are great solutions.

Advertise like crazy: It's an expensive endeavor to take an undifferentiated commodity and convince the market to buy yours. And, with ever savvier consumers, it's harder now than ever. Consumer research demonstrates that brands mean less than ever as an increasing majority agree with the statement "Brand names are not better quality." Even if you succeed, like the branded examples above, you'll need to raise your prices to pay for all that advertising (which, by the way, isn't an option if you accept insurance).

Cut prices: Reduce prices and you begin a race to the bottom. How cheap can you make your paperclips? You *can* win on price, but your margins will be razor thin. Also, there always seems to be someone willing to provide a lesser product for just a little cheaper. Perhaps that's why my paperclips break when I bend them—someone must have realized it's a fraction of a cent cheaper to manufacture brittle paperclips.

Be Different or Die

The statement "be different or die" is dramatic. To be fair, it should probably read "be different or run a mediocre company, with declining profit margins, that sells an undifferentiated commodity" (you'd almost prefer death, right?). To avoid this fate, your practice needs to be different from the competition. That said, you don't need to modify your core service of counseling.

Take for example, paint. Paint is a commodity. Give me any color from any brand and it can be matched exactly. Moreover, once the paint is on the wall, nobody can tell me if it's Behr or Sherman Williams. However, Dutch Boy had a huge success when they released easy pour twist top paint cans. They were even able to raise their prices! Was the new design for everyone? Not at all. Plenty of people balked at the higher price, and contractors and professional painters don't care whether their paint cans have a screw on lid. But for some consumers, it was a smash hit.

Like Dutch Boy, think of how your practice can be *notably* different from your competition. A refurbished office won't cut it—you need an extreme makeover. A friendly staff won't do it either—the service needs to be shocking. Having evening hours isn't enough—to stand out you'll need amazing hours, walk-in sessions, or terrible hours. You can't be a couple notches better or worse, you need to go choose a direction and go all the way to the end of the belt. Here are some ideas:

- Counseling marketing materials are usually bright and cheery. Why not go dark? Why not have everything from your website to your business cards reflect clients' dark moods? Make them black, with gray font.

- Counseling marketing materials can be a little cheesy. Make yours over-the-top cheesy. "Come to XYZ Counseling center, where everyone is special." "We accept most major insurance plans. How does that make you feel?" Just make sure that clients know you're in on the joke.

- Create a full-fledged coffee bar where people pay for their session, and also get an Americano. Punch a card—10 sessions and the 11th is free—just like at a coffee shop.

- Go frou frou. Sequenced pillows. Pink faux fur armchairs. US Weekly. Men will hate it. The design caters exclusively to a certain type of woman.

- After each session, the client gets an emailed summary from you reviewing what you covered in session and the client's homework for the week.

- Build a library (at least a full wall of shelves) at your practice where clients can sign out books and CDs.

- Create an unusual policy: If you cancel a session with less than 24 hours' notice, you pay the client your no-show fee!

- Cater to the medical marijuana community, and talk about how different strains of cannabis can help with insomnia, or other mental health issues.

- Everyone in your office dresses in athletic wear akin to personal trainers at the gym. Make the whole practice gym themed, renaming therapy concepts to sound like physical exercises.

Clearly some of these ideas are pushing the envelope—and that's exactly the point! **Think in extremes:** Bright/Dark, Strict/Flexible, Happy/Sad, 'Judgy'/Companionate, Masculine/Feminine, Modern/Classical, Hot/Cold, Colorful/Greyscale, Hard/Soft, Casual/Formal, Loud/Quiet, Artistic/Straight-forward, Natural/Synthetic, Disposable/Permanent, Electronic/Unplugged. Will your concept appeal to everyone? Heck no! But you're never going to win an entire market no matter what you do. Instead, for those that your concept appeals to, your practice will be more talked about, and highly sought after, because your practice is unique and different from the competition. You have successfully differentiated your company.

Isn't it About the Counseling?

One thing you'll notice is that none of these ideas effect your core service. Your business cards might be black, but your sessions are still in color. Your office might have overstuffed brown leather chairs and a masculine feel, but there are still tissues for those who need them.

Every year in NYC hundreds of restaurants with great food fail. The answer isn't always make better food. The answer might be to call your restaurant "Ninja", dress your servers like Ninjas and have them startle the bejesus out of your guests while they try to eat Sushi. Is it for everyone? No. Last time I was in New York, did I go there for dinner? No comment.

Lesson 34:
Private Practice and Social Marketing

It's hard to get people to talk about your business...if you're a restaurant. If you're a counselor, you're really fighting an uphill battle, as clients need to overcome the social stigma of being in counseling in order to tell others about your service.

Therefore, to recruit a "raving fan" (that is, someone who passionately tells others about your service), you have to make a big positive impression. You have to exceed your clients' expectations, provide outstanding service and care, and offer a "remarkable" experience that they can't help but to tell their friends about.

Once you accomplish this, and you have clients who are talking about you, or writing blogs about you, or posting reviews about you, or maybe even singing songs about you (who knows?), there is something very important that you need to do.

Ready?

This is what you need to do: Stay Out Of Their Way!
It took a lot of fuel to get that car moving...don't hit the brakes!

The only reason you should intervene is to help, encourage, reward, thank, or incentivize your fans to continue talking about (thereby promoting) your counseling service.

It should be Common Sense Not to Hush your Cheerleaders, but...

Businesses make mistakes all the time as they try to manage their fans, and control the way that their fans share their brand. For sure, your customers won't market your counseling practice the way you market your counseling practice. They will do it their way — in chat rooms, on a blog, in unscrupulous terms to their friends.

- They might quote you without permission.
- They might copy text from your brochure.
- They might copy and paste your logo.
- They might take a picture of your office, and tag it on Facebook.

A client could mention that you wore an ugly sweater on Wednesday (my clients have told others that I wear brightly colored socks. Not exactly what my marketing message is, but I'll take it! And I feel fortunate that my clients are talking about my practice).

Learn to love your clients' creative and unorthodox methods of spreading the word about your service. Learn to get comfortable being reviewed: even if reviews are mixed. Even some of the reviews are negative (and some will be).

A Real Life Example of What Not to Do

I had been promoting a company (let's call them "Company X") in my writing, speaking, and consulting for a couple of years. Recently, I copied an email they had sent me about an upcoming sale, and posted it online to share with my readers in hopes of sending Company X more customers,

Sounds good, right? Not to the marketing department at Company X. 24 hours after posting the email, a company representative contacted me to request that I remove the post. Here's the email I received:

***

Hi Anthony!

I hope this email finds you well. I was doing some searching on the internet and noticed you posted up our entire Black Friday email on your WordPress blog www.startacounselingpractice.com This was a special offer sent out only to our previous customers, and not intended to be posted up for the public to see. I would appreciate it if you removed the coupon code and email entirely. Thanks so much
and please let me know if you have any other questions.

[Name Removed]

Director

_____

[Company Name Removed]

***

This is a polite email, for sure, but it's the opposite message you want to send to anyone trying to send your business. If Company X was smart about getting the word out about their product, the staff would have sent me more offers to promote. Instead, they couldn't handle that my promotion approach was different from theirs! How unfortunate! Don't make this mistake with your clients.

More Resources on Marketing a Counseling Practice

I'm going to be writing on this topic more, but for now, let me recommend a few books that could help you market your small businesses / counseling practice:

- "What Would Google Do," by Jeff Jarvis
- "Raving Fans," by Ken Blanchard
- "The Gift Economy," By Gary Vanerchuck
- "The Referral Generator," John Jantsch

Lesson 35:
How to Prevent and Manage Negative Online Reviews

Today, it is easier than ever for clients to vocalize their personal experiences with your practice. Online destinations such as Yelp, Google Places, Insider Pages, Foursquare, Gowalla and the BBB (Better Business Bureau) provide easy ways for consumers to write reviews on everything from restaurants to therapists.

In addition to online review sites, many individuals today manage their own websites and blogs where they write at length about their life experiences. Blogger Jeff Jarvis used his site BuzzMachine to vent about his trouble with Dell's products and customer service, sparking a huge online discussion known as "Dell's Hell." The page became so popular that it showed up on Google when people searched "Dell computers," and the negative online press damaged the company's reputation and sales.

Online press is a double-edged sword. On one hand, there is opportunity for excellent reviews that boost business. On the other, negative press can be deadly — and it's an inconvenient fact that people are more likely to report negative experiences than good ones. Hence, no practice is immune to negative online press from clients. You might not have a website, a Facebook account or even a computer, but your clients do. In fact, the question isn't if someone will write something negative, but when — and how will you handle it?

Fill the vacuum

On the Internet, the only thing worse than negative reviews is having those reviews published in a vacuum. Managers need to take control of the conversation about their companies in advance of any negativity. Here are some strategies one can begin using immediately.

1) Solicit online reviews.

Counselors recoil at this suggestion. Some say it's inappropriate, some say it's unethical, and some say their clients simply won't stand for it. None of this is true, of course. There is nothing unethical about tactfully (and without pressure or threat of penalty) informing your clients that people today are searching online to find counselors and that an online review could help other potential clients connect with your practice. In fact, if you have been doing good work with your clients, some of them may be wondering how they can help you in return.

2) Compete for awards and accolades.

Winning an award or accolade is like a positive review on steroids. When a potential client sees that your practice was "Voted best of Portsmouth by Harbor Magazine 2010!" he or she will have increased confidence in your brand. Many publications issue "best of"-type awards to local businesses in a variety of categories. To begin, contact local publications to inquire about the nomination process (perhaps they don't have a category for counseling — yet!).

3) Seek professional endorsements.

Ask other health professionals who know your work to provide two- to three-sentence endorsements. You can publish these blurbs on your website, accompanied by the professionals' pictures and full names, to help build credibility. This level of identification is golden in a world in which unscrupulous companies create fake reviews by fictitious customers ("You changed my life, thanks! — Jake, NYC").

4) Own your search results.

When people search your business name online, make sure every result on the first page of Google is one you control or have contributed to. How? Publish quality web content: articles, videos, press releases and blogs. Also set up a Facebook page, Twitter page, Google Places page, LinkedIn page and maybe even a Myspace page. This level of online saturation is important because when someone does finally post something negative about you, their negative comment could be so far down on the search results that new potential clients won't see it.

5) Tell your company's story.

Telling your company's story will help you to build trust with potential new clients. Your story isn't a one-time history of your company; it's an evolving narrative about who you are, what you're working on and how you're active within your community.

Note: If you don't have anything to write about, then you're not doing enough!

Responding to upset client-customers

Great customer service will reduce client complaints, but it will never eliminate them. All businesses get upset customers. Like all companies, you will make mistakes, and (let's be honest) sometimes customers are difficult to please. Here's what to do when you learn that you have an angry client-customer.

6) Apologize for their experience.

Some counselors have a bad habit of taking a client's negative experience and making it a clinical issue. A client will say, "I'm mad that you were late to our appointment," and the therapist will respond, "Who do I remind you of when you feel like that?" Client complaints are often legitimate customer service issues, plain and simple. Hence, it is appropriate to apologize for clients' negative service experiences — even if they are wrong! Perhaps you've heard of the customer service legend surrounding Nordstrom. In one account, a sales clerk refunded a customer for a set of car tires, even though Nordstrom has never sold tires! How does your customer service stack up?

7) Listen to their story.

Like any customer, angry clients want to be heard. When clients are angry, thank them for the opportunity to learn from their negative experience and then let them talk (off the clock!). Then ask them to tell you more. And then more. And then more! Make sure these clients tell you their whole story — every perception and feeling about it. Then say, "Now that I know your entire experience, how can I make things right?" After being heard in person, clients will feel less compulsion to rehash their complaints online (plus they'll appreciate your patient listening).

8) Set the bar high.

I called my bank the other day, and the attendant answering the phone said, "Thanks for calling Bank of America. How can I exceed your expectations today?" Wow, you just did! Let clients know that your goal is to exceed their expectations. By setting the bar high, if you miss your objective, perhaps you will simply meet their expectations, which is not bad for a "miss."

9) Respond to online criticisms politely and directly.

Some consumer sites give business owners the opportunity to respond publicly to customer reviews. Take advantage of this! When someone writes a negative review or comment about your practice, respond in a positive and professional way. Consider that while a negative review may hurt sales in the short-term, the constructive criticism gives your company an opportunity to learn and improve for the long-term.

Quality and reputation

The preceding "heavy-duty" strategies will help to strengthen and protect your company's reputation. One word of caution, however. No matter how savvy a business is with reputation management, if the food tastes bad, the restaurant will eventually fail. Hence, these strategies work best when combined with exceptional customer service and quality clinical care.

Lesson 36:
Improving Client Retention: 7 Ethical Strategies

As professional counselors, we help others. It's in our DNA, our personalities, and our extensive training. This is usually a good thing. However, it has its dark side too. Over the last 10 years, I have noticed an alarming reluctance among counselors to run their practices so that they benefit their clients AND manage to keep themselves in business. It's as if counselors have the motto: "If it's good for me, it's probably bad for my clients—and it's also probably unethical."

For example, I have consulted with counselors who have tens of thousands of dollars in uncollected fees, because they can't bring themselves to ask their clients for the money they owe. I've heard providers say, "I'm their counselor. It's uncomfortable to take money from someone I'm supposed to be helping." Some counselors even try to make a case that taking money from clients hurts their treatment.

Secondly, I have been meeting with counselors who have poor client retention. According to their caseloads, it seems to them that clients today are staying in treatment for shorter and shorter durations of time, and attending sessions less consistently than ever before. Forget the brief therapy model of 12 sessions—some of their clients average as little as 7 sessions or less (surprisingly, those clients are often not made aware that an ultra-short stint in therapy doesn't mean they're "all better," and isn't recommended by even the briefest therapy models).

Client retention is an ethical issue. But for the vast majority, the issue is not about the ethics of manipulating clients to stay in treatment (which is what some counselors think "client retention" is); rather it's becoming an ethical issue around not providing adequate and complete treatment to clients. If you think you and your clients could benefit from more sessions together, here are 7 ethical strategies for improving client retention:

1) Familiarize Clients to a Suitable Course of Treatment

Counselors need to educate clients about what constitutes a typical course of treatment. Consider this:

A few years ago, I was having some neck and shoulder pain, so I paid a visit to a local chiropractor. During my first consultation, even before my first chiro-adjustment, my chiropractor asked me how often I planned on coming in. I answered that I was thinking I would come in once a week.

She responded, "Well, I won't turn you away if you want to come in just once a week. However, you're not going to see the benefits you're hoping for unless you come in at least 2 or even 3 times a week, for at least the first couple of months. I will probably need to readjust your back every few days, to make any lasting improvements."

I appreciated the information. Had I been left to my own devices, I would have wrongly assumed that once a week would be enough. We agreed on two sessions a week for the first 6 weeks, and scheduled a re-evaluation appointment for 6 weeks later.

Unfortunately, when it comes to educating therapy clients about a recommended frequency or duration of treatment, counselors often resist—because they are wary of manipulating or strong-arming clients (a potentially needless worry, since, in actuality we rarely have that much influence!).

Wacky Counselor Statements:

"I let new clients decide how often they come in, and I try not to influence their decision."

"I think clients know how often they need to see me."

"It's unethical to tell clients how often I think they should see me for therapy."

2) Familiarize Clients to a Suitable Course of Treatment—AGAIN

My orientation to chiropractic medicine didn't end at the beginning of my first session. After my first session, I was given a bag of goodies ranging from coupons for chiropractic products to a local massage therapist, to samples of a therapeutic sports cream. Also in the bag was a small book titled "Chicken Soup for the Chiropractic Soul."

The book contained a number of stories about people with back pain or posture issues, who sought chiropractic help for their ailments. The stories illustrated—in inspirational detail—how, after many sessions, patients' backs became straighter, stronger, and healthier, and how their pain went away.

In retrospect, I am sure that the stories from this book encouraged me to stay in treatment on days when I wasn't feeling particularly motivated.

Wacky Counselor Statements:

"During the first appointment, I try to convince the clients not to come back."

"The problem is that clients are ambivalent about whether or not they want to be in counseling."

"If clients don't continue treatment, they must not be ready to change."

3) Familiarize Clients to a Suitable Course of Treatment—AGAIN, and AGAIN, and AGAIN...

As my chiropractic treatment progressed, one thing I noticed was that my chiropractor actively encouraged me to continue treatment, and noted my progress regularly (which served as encouragement to continue). When I sat in the waiting room (usually for only a couple minutes—therapists take note), I would look up at a framed print on the wall. It read, "Every session builds on the last" and contained an image of a bricklayer, hardhat and all, building a brick wall, one brick at a time. I laughed a couple times at the cliché, but I also got the message.

The Message: Every appointment was getting me incrementally— sometimes recognizably so and sometimes less recognizably—toward my goal.

I tell this story to counselors, and they cringe. "The doctor actively encouraged you to continue treatment? Didn't you feel taken advantage of? Didn't you feel like a meal ticket?"

My answer has been and will continue to be "Not at all!" In contrast, I felt that I was getting excellent service and a high quality of care. Sure, the doctor was making money from my sessions, but I was getting what I came for—a positive treatment outcome.

Important Note: For me, arguably a pretty motivated patient, a positive outcome necessitated not just great chiropractic care, but also regular encouragement to keep me coming back for more care and continued care. Might counseling clients need such encouragement too?

Wacky Counselor Statements:

"A good number of clients can be finished with counseling after 5 or 6 sessions."

"The client I saw today only needed 1 session."

Above, we investigated the importance of familiarizing clients to a suitable frequency and duration of treatment (steps 1-3). This lesson concludes our review of this topic with the final 4 strategies for improving client retention.

4) Don't Practice a Strict "Disorder Model" of Care

Counseling isn't just about mental illness and psychological disorders. It's about helping clients to live exciting, fulfilling lives.

Over the last 30 years, counselors have become focused on a very medical model of care, where treating/resolving a diagnosable mental disorder is the goal of treatment. This approach has paved the way for "life coaches" (usually providers without the clinical expertise and training of licensed counselors) to walk on the scene and become the new "people helpers" of choice. Somewhere, Carl Rogers is rolling in his grave.

If your clients are alive, they are changing, and they are growing. Even the lives of the healthiest persons have stress, difficult challenges, and can benefit from support and counseling.

Wacky Counselor Statements:

"We had little to talk about in therapy this week, which tells me that we must be finished with counseling."

"When it seems we're not making progress after a session or two, I suggest clients take a break from counseling."

5) Break the "See you Next Week" Mold

This seems like common sense, but many counselors are so used to seeing clients once a week (or every other week) that the idea of seeing a client 2, 3, or more times in a week sounds like Spanish (or extortion) to them.

The truth is, you probably have clients who could genuinely benefit from more than one session a week, especially (but not limited to) clients at the beginning of treatment. If you're like many of the counselors I consult with, perhaps you haven't even offered this!

Wacky Counselor Statements:

"None of my clients want to see me more than once a week."
"I'm not a psychoanalyst. I can't see clients more than once a week."

6) Don't Terminate Too Early

Recently, I was supervising a therapist who had a client presenting some commitment issues. The client had been dating a woman for a number of years, and while he loved the woman, he feared taking the next step toward marriage.

I was surprised when just a couple weeks later, the counselor I was supervising reported that he had terminated therapy with the client, as they had completed their therapy goals. The supervisee explained, "We talked about it in session, and he's over his commitment issues. He says he's ready to move forward."

"Really?" I said. "Did he buy a ring?"

"Um. No."

"He's proposed?"

The supervisee laughed in spite of himself.

"Haha, no. I didn't think of that. Maybe we're not done after all."

This client wasn't finished with counseling—he was just getting started! Counselors need to remember how important client action is to completing treatment, and that there's going to almost always be regression as a part of growth progress. Surely, this client was likely to have new feelings of anxiety when he began to take actions toward establishing a more committed relationship.

When counselors terminate therapy too early, the message to the client is, "You should be better now. If you're not—maybe there's something seriously wrong with you that counseling can't help you with."

Wacky Counselor Statements

(See counselor's half of dialogue above.)

7) Follow Up with Clients Who Have Lost Touch

Last but not least is the issue of following up with clients after they have left or "completed" care.

There are a lot of reasons that counseling treatment can get interrupted: Seasonal illness, vacations and holidays, scheduling problems, car trouble, work conflicts, etc.

When clients get out of the habit of coming in for counseling, it can spell the end of treatment. For example, have you ever gone to the gym consistently, only to have your routine broken by some external event? It can take a long time to get back on the treadmill.

I have found that counselors are very reluctant to call clients. They worry that they will be bothering their clients, violating their sense of privacy, or that they will seem pushy. I have found that this is almost never the case. In fact, the opposite seems to be true. When it's sincere, clients deeply appreciate getting a phone call from their "doctor" (and as their counselor, that's you).

I can recall numerous instances where counselors I worked with were literally terrified to follow up with a client by telephone. We often had a good laugh when they finally overcame their fear, dialed the phone, and was profusely thanked by their client for the call (and rewarded with a new appointment on the books!).

Don't worry about being seen as insincere, because you're not! You're a caring and thoughtful therapist, who wants to reconnect with your clients to promote their success. Also, consider this: your client usually pays to talk with you. Now, you're calling to talk with them at no charge—how is that not fantastic?

A simple call like this will suffice:

1. Say, "Hi [Jamie] this is [Anthony, from Thrive]. I'm calling because I haven't seen you since the [winter storm], and I wanted to see how you're doing.

2. [Active Listening to client response].

3. Say, "When we left off, we were making progress toward our treatment goals, but were not yet finished. Shall we get started again this week?"

Wacky Counselor Statements:

"I'm worried that a phone call would be a nuisance to my clients."

"My clients will be 'creeped out' if I call them."

"My client is an adult and should call me if he/she wants to continue seeing me."

"Win-win" is Not a Dirty Word

Will it benefit you if your clients come to counseling more regularly, and have more sessions with you? Absolutely. You might even grow a full and profitable practice. Will better client retention improve treatment outcomes for your clients? Without question it will. It's a win-win.

Lesson 37:
Prepare Clients for These 9 Therapy Issues

A Focus on Counseling Client Education

Expectations are everything; and getting buy-in for how things work at your practice is an important part of facilitating happy, satisfied, clients. However, too often client education and informed consent resembles the oft-ignored "terms of use" contract in iTunes. Clients are handed a sheet with 2,000 words of 10-point text and asked to sign (or click "I agree") to move forward.

This month, we'll review nine areas where client education is imperative **Additionally, you can click here to learn more about opening your own Thriveworks Counseling franchise.**

1. The Wait to Get an Appointment

Walt Disney World has long lines, but no one revolts — guests are prepared in advance for the inconvenience. In fact, despite the crowds and wait times (and high prices), Disney has extremely high guest satisfaction ratings.

Emulate Disney and **be up front with clients** about how long it can take to get scheduled at your practice. At my centers, we get new clients in the door quickly (within 24 hours) for their first appointment. However, we've learned that we also need to educate clients that (1) the wait times for some specific counselors can be weeks (or longer), and (2) if one fails to schedule regularly with their counselor, that counselor could become fully booked with other clients.

2. If Insurance Doesn't Pay, the Client is Responsible for All Fees

Some counseling practices gloss over this detail and then have conflict with clients when a billing issue occurs. If you accept insurance, spend time with clients before their first session and talk through the insurance billing process. **It's okay to disclose what you expect insurance to pay**.

> *"However, clients need to know that if insurance falls short the conflict over the difference isn't between your practice and him/her; it's between the client and his/her insurance company."*

In a recent trip to my Primary Care Provider (PCP), insurance didn't cover as much as we all expected. Because we had discussed the possibility, I paid the difference (with some disdain for my insurance provider, but not for my PCP).

3. The No Show / Late Cancelation Fee

In any given week, a 20 percent cancellation rate isn't unprecedented for a mental health counseling practice. Still, late cancellation fees become "fine print" when counselors don't want to talk about them. By avoiding the issue early on, one sets the stage for many awkward conversations down the road (spoiler alert, the issue is going to come up—a lot!).

Instead, **inform your clients about your late cancellation and no-show policy**, or suffer the consequences of clients who believe that missing a session "every once in a while" shouldn't come at a cost. Also, disclose the fee prominently via a sign in your waiting room.

4. A Realistic Duration of Treatment

People want quick fixes, and sometimes counselors are worried about scaring off new clients if they communicate that meaningful change takes time. This reluctance doesn't help anyone. When treatment duration isn't understood, individuals and couples might drop out after three to five sessions saying, "Well, I/we gave counseling a try. It didn't work."

Instead, **inform clients that brief therapy starts at around 10 sessions**, and some clients will need additional sessions to reach their treatment goals.

5. Sessions Can Be Difficult

Do you know of any counselors who waste sessions "shooting the breeze" with their clients and, instead of bothering with the hard work of therapy, mollify their clients on every issue?

We've all had clients who have said, "my last counselor never challenged me", or "my last counselor just sat and listened to me." Make sure that this isn't the expectation of new clients. In your office, **clients make progress — and that takes hard work**.

6. Limits to Confidentiality

It might be old hat to you, but it's not to your clients. Taking time to go through the limits of confidentiality is both an ethical obligation and a way to **show your clients that you respect them enough to inform them** of the laws.

7. Treatment Record Ownership

For most adult clients this is pretty well understood. However, when it comes to children or couples/family sessions, **it's more imperative to explain to clients the ground rules**. For couples, I've found that section 2.2 of the AAMFT Code of Ethics does a nice job of determining whom the record belongs to — both clients execute a release, or nobody gets them.

8. Getting Stuck is Okay

Getting "stuck" is a common phenomenon in the counseling process. Inform your clients of this, and also that **not having much to say in session isn't a sign that you're "done with counseling."** It's a signal to keep working because something is blocking your progress.

9. Things Will Get Better

Hope is a powerful thing. Prepare your clients that the silver lining will get longer, the light at the end of the tunnel will get brighter, and that pain will pass in time.

A client experiencing an issue like bereavement or major depression might have little hope and think, "I'll never fully recover." You know this isn't true; so make sure you tell the client!

When a potential client reaches out for counseling, it's normal to want to get started without any delay. However, taking the time to prepare an inquirer for what being a client is like at your practice is an important part of that person's (and your) ultimate success.

Lesson 38:
A Real Solution to Client No-shows and Late Cancellations

You are a counselor in private practice. You work 5 days a week, booking yourself 6 clients a day. You could schedule more, but you feel that 30 sessions is a good fulltime caseload. However, at the end of each week you review your caseload and notice that, again, you had only 25 sessions. What gives?

If you're like many counselors, you are no stranger to last-minute client cancellations and no-shows. These events hurt your practice, worsen clients' treatment outcomes, and put a monkey wrench in your schedule.

But Wait, you Have a No-show Policy!

Almost all counselors have a no-show policy. Still, counselors are often reluctant to enforce their policies—in part because their clients haven't fully bought into them. Do the following counselor statements resonate with you? "Jane, she's a good client, and this is the first time she's cancelled late." "Rob, he gave 23 hours' notice, even though I didn't fill the gap in my schedule, that's really close to my 24-hour policy." "Erin, she says she has a fever of 102 degrees. She's seriously sick!" "Dave has no excuse for missing his appointment, but he swears that I never told him my policy, and he'll quit therapy and slam me online if I charge him."

A New Approach to your No-show Policy

Every counseling student learns that there is a difference between *signed* consent and *informed* consent; a client might sign a consent form but if he or she never read it, there is no informed consent. Hence, counselors regularly read through their consent forms with clients.

However, I think that consent needs to be taken a step further. In addition to *informed* consent, counselors need to obtain *client agreement and buy in.*

The Typical No-Show / Cancelation Policy Review

Counselors typically rush through the informed consent process. There is a lot of incentive to do this: Clients, during a first appointment, are typically not in their best emotional place, and counselors want to deliver value in the first appointment, not legalese. Hence, a no-show policy review might sound like this:

> *"Now that we've spoken about confidentiality, let's talk cancellation policy: I have a 24-hour cancellation policy. I will need to charge you for an appointment if you don't give me at least 24 hours' notice. Now let's talk about my duty to report..."*

Is this clear? Maybe. But it's not memorable. It doesn't address whether there are any exceptions to the rule. It doesn't emphasize how serious you are about enforcing the policy. It doesn't provide a rationale as to why you have a cancelation policy. A client will hear your policy and she might even remember it, but she will perhaps never truly buy into it. To keep the session moving forward, the client will sign your form and hand it back to you. Then, the day you try and enforce your cancellation policy will be the day you'll learn how little consent you really obtained from your client. As one client recently said "...it is unfair and unjust. I understand policies, but I work for a living, so when I am told I must work, then I MUST WORK!"[1]

---

[1] A slightly modified direct quote from an anonymous client.

For many practices, client retaliation to cancellation fees is the norm, not the exception. Something needs to change!

The Over-the-top No-show / Cancellation Policy Review

In the title, I described the cancellation policy procedure below as "over-the-top," "legalistic," and even "unforgiving," but it is really none of the three. Below is simply a sample model on how to clearly and thoroughly communicate your policy to clients and make sure you obtain the essential client buy-in you need. Here it goes:

"Karen, before we get started, I need to talk with you about my cancellation and no-show policy. I want to make sure that there's no miscommunication about it, and that you understand it and agree to it 100%.

My cancellation policy is this: Clients can cancel or reschedule an appointment anytime, as long as they provide 24 hours' notice. If you cancel an appointment with less than 24 hours' notice, or fail to show up, you will be charged for the appointment.

Some practices have a 48-hour policy. Some even have a 72-hour policy. Mine is 24 hours, and I am firm at 24 hours.

This cancellation policy is really important for my counseling practice because, while a medical doctor can see 35 patients in a day, a therapist like me generally sees a maximum of 6 or 7. I reserve for you, and all my clients, a full hour of my time for the session and clinical notes. If a client cancels with less than a full 24-hour notice, I won't be able to fill that time slot, and I'll lose an entire hour from my work schedule.

I want you to know that my cancellation policy in not a penalty or a punishment. Ninety-nine point nine percent of my clients understand this. Very rarely, I'll have a client who will feel that he or she is being punished when I charge them a late cancellation fee. I want to make sure that you don't feel this way, if someday you miss an appointment. Truth be told, if you are in counseling long enough, at some point you might forget about an appointment, or something will come up in your schedule that will result in you missing an appointment. Maybe you'll need to work late. Maybe you'll get a sudden onset of the flu. Maybe your kids will have doctor appointments, or your car will break down, or something unavoidable will come up.

I'm never upset with clients when they miss an appointment. I know that's life. In return, my clients understand that scheduling an appointment with me is like buying tickets to an event. If you miss the event, it doesn't matter why you missed it, or even if it was your first time, you can't turn in your tickets for a refund.

Also, our late cancellation and no-show fee is $99. It's important to remember that insurance will not pay for missed appointments, so you will be responsible for the full $99, not just a co-pay.

The fact that I'm spending so much time talking about this might seem like overkill—thanks for bearing with me! I am fortunate in that my clients are fully on board with this policy, and this makes life so much easier for my clients and me.

So, Karen, in order to move forward, I need from you, not just your consent but also your enthusiastic agreement and promise, that if or when the day comes that you miss an appointment, for any reason, you will gladly pay for the missed appointment, just like you pay for the sessions you attend. *Do I have your agreement and promise?"*

Buy-in is Mandatory

After giving this—or a similar—explanation of your cancellation policy, and after ending it with a request for "enthusiastic agreement," pause and wait for the client to answer. If the client agrees verbally at this point, it is likely that he/she has truly agreed to your policy, and that you will never need to worry about problems charging for missed appointments or late cancellations.

Some clients will not agree. A client might say, "That seems a little too inflexible to me. If I have to stay at work late, or my kids get sick, I can't control that and I don't have the finances to pay for sessions I'm not attending." In these instances, kindly reply, "I completely understand. The value of the consent process is that both you and I can see if my services are going to be a good fit. I cannot move forward, but I do have a list of other providers who might be a better fit for you at this time." Then, let the would-be client leave.

While such a policy may on the surface sound over-the-top, extreme, legalistic or even unforgiving, in actuality, sharing expectations from the first session will ultimately go a long way to build trust and a solid therapeutic relationship with your clients.

Lesson 39:
Protecting Client Privacy in the Electronic Age

Recently, my wife, daughter and I visited the Smithsonian National Museum of American History, in Washington, DC. In taking a history tour of U.S. presidents, an exhibit about Richard Nixon stood out. On display was a metal filing cabinet that had been pried open. An explanation nearby read, *"The Nixon administration established a secret-operations unit known as the Plumbers. On September 3, 1971, they broke into the office of Dr. Lewis Fielding, Daniel Ellsberg's psychiatrist. They were looking for damaging information..."*

> As I looked back at the torn filing cabinet, I thought, *"back then, before everything was electronic, someone could break into an office and steal a patient's file. Today, someone can break in to a database and steal millions of patient files."*

We're at Risk...Because Data is Electronic

As Counselors, we care about our clients, and protecting client privacy is a priority. We make sure that our offices are soundproofed, we received signed permission for any Personal Health Information (PHI) being released, we challenge subpoena's for client records, and we dutifully "can neither confirm nor deny" whether so-and-so is a client. The trust we keep with our clients is sacrosanct. However, counselors today are facing a new challenge, which includes securing electronic data and communications. And while counselors are responsible (and held accountable) for securing this electronic information, the resources available with which to defend it are inadequate.

A decade ago, people were worried about online security. Some even thought that electronic data would jeopardize people's privacy, and increase susceptibility to identity theft. *They were right!* Today, it is estimated that 1 in 5 persons in the U.S. has been a victim of identity theft.

In 2009, Steve Ballmer, Microsoft CEO, described the need for better cyber security, stating, *"The president needs to use his 'bully pulpit' to make sure businesses and local governments are protecting their data."* Despite new legislation that penalizes companies (and clinicians) who suffer a data breach, the situation poses a dilemma for clinicians because—while penalties are securely in place—ironclad methods for ensuring security are not available.

We're at Risk...Because 2011 Brought the Worst Data Breaches of All Time

A report from the Privacy Rights Clearinghouse (PRC) notes 535 breaches in 2011, involving 30.4 million sensitive records (that's a low estimate, as many data breaches go un-reported). Here are some highlights:

Sony.

Sony suffered more than 12 breaches in 2011, effecting over 100 million customer records, including passwords. Hence, any customer who reuses their passwords is at future risk, as hackers can use his/her stolen password to access said customer's non-Sony accounts.

Sutter Physicians Services.

Data from Sutter Physicians Services was breached when a thief stole a desktop computer, which contained about 3.3 million patients' medical details.

Epsilon.

Moderate estimates reveal 60 million customer email addresses were stolen from Epsilon.

Tricare.

The data of 5.1 million people were stolen from the car of a Tricare employee (medical and financial information). The breach has led to a $4.9 billion lawsuit.

Nasdaq.

Hackers accessed a cloud-based Nasdaq system called "Director's Desk" that facilitates boardroom-level conferences for 10,000 executives. By monitoring communications, hackers had access to valuable insider-trading information (wouldn't you like to be a fly on the wall during those conversations?).[2]

Some of the above breaches were the product of negligence (as in the case of unsecured data), and some were the result of sophisticated attacks. Still, both pose an important question: If Sony, NASDAQ, and Tricare can't protect their data, can counselors in private practice be expected to do better?

---

[2] http://www.informationweek.com/news/security/attacks/232301079

We're at Risk...Because of Standard Operating Procedures

Today, a clinician can be vigilant about PHI security, and still fall short. One small error: losing a flash drive, failing to logout of a program, or forgetting to "blind carbon copy" an email can lead to a serious HIPAA violation.

Indeed, even standard practices are risky. For example, if a practice receives an electronic fax that contains PHI, that fax is unencrypted and therefore at risk. If a client sends an email asking for confirmation of their appointment time, a simple "yes or no" response could lead to a HIPAA violation, as you are identifying the person as a patient (and email communication is not encrypted). According to Nancy Wheeler, JD, while it isn't illegal to use email to communicate with clients, the clinician is liable if there is a security breach.[3] Put simply, many of us are rolling the dice every day.

We're at Risk...Even if we're Flawless

If you commit to never send an email, never receive an electronic fax, and to surgically attach your laptop to your, well, lap, therein making it impenetrable to theft, sorry...you're still doomed.

We're at Risk...Because We Use Passwords

The most common way that hackers get into protected systems is by guessing the password (By the way, the most common password for businesses is "Password1," which satisfies the industry-standard complexity rules—9 characters including an upper-case letter and a number). Today, hackers can use brute-force techniques to simply cycle through all possible character combinations. Even eight-character passwords, with more than 6 quadrillion possibilities, are short work. Using a $1,500 computer built with

---

[3] A presentation at the Virginia Counselors Association Conference, 2011.

off-the-shelf parts, it took Trustwave (a security company) just 10 hours to harvest a cache of 200,000 passwords. Also, as part of Trustwave's "2012 Global Security Report," they tried to crack 2.5 million passwords. They came close, successfully cracking more than 2.1 million in their study.[4]

What do we do? Passwords are intrinsically flawed as a security method, but they are—in practicality—what we are dealt to protect our, and our clients, most private information. More advanced solutions such as biometric authentication, smartcards, and one-time key generators show greater promise,[5] but they are all but unavailable for general consumer use.

We're at Risk... Because Even Google is Hacked!

Not even the almighty Google is safe. In March of 2012, a Russian university student hacked into Google's Chrome web browser. The good news is that this was a contest, and the student won $60,000 for the exploit.[6] The bad news is that the hack was so good that all a user needed to do was to visit an infected website using Google Chrome. Without so much as downloading a malicious plug-in, the hacker gained complete access to the victim's computer!

Such attacks occur in the real world. Moreover, a Verizon study revealed that hackers are often inside victims' networks for months or years before being

---

[4] http://money.cnn.com/2012/03/01/technology/password_security/index.htm

[5] ibid.

[6] http://www.zdnet.com/blog/security/cansecwest-pwnium-google-chrome-hacked-with-sandbox-bypass/10563

discovered; and more than two-thirds of companies learn they've been attacked only after an external party notifies them.

We're at Risk...Because of Social Penalties

Penalties for clinicians who fail to protect client privacy are severe. According to the U.S. Department of Health and Human Services, *"As required by section 13402(e)(4) of the HITECH Act, the Secretary must post a list of breaches of unsecured protected health information affecting 500 or more individuals. These breaches are now posted in a new, more accessible format that allows users to search and sort the posted breaches. Additionally, this new format includes brief summaries of the breach cases that OCR has investigated and closed, as well as the names of private practice providers..."*[7]

Simply put, if there is an attack on your system and the information of 500 or more individuals is compromised, not only do you need to notify effected clients (which, appropriately so, needs to be done with any breach) your practice also gets added to the "hall of shame." Moreover, this list is available on numerous websites across the web.[8]

We're at Risk...Because of Civil and Financial Penalties

The "American Recovery and Reinvestment Act of 2009" has established a tiered penalty structure for HIPAA violations.

---

[7]http://www.hhs.gov/ocr/privacy/hipaa/administrative/breachnotificationrule/breachtool.html

[8] http://www.uia.net/hitech-breaches

For example, in the case of a HIPAA violation, wherein an Individual did not know (and by exercising reasonable diligence would not have known) that he/she violated HIPAA, there exists a potential maximum penalty of $50,000 per violation, with an annual maximum of $1.5 million (and a minimum penalty of $100). In addition, penalties get higher in instances of "reasonable cause," "willful neglect," and when violations what are not corrected. [9]

We're at Risk...But We're Not Doomed

While it might not be possible to guarantee client privacy, we can provide some security—even decent security. Here are some tips:

1. Make sure that, if a computer is stolen, there isn't unsecured data on it.

2. Make sure that passwords are at least 9 characters, and include a combination of capital letters, lowercase letters, and numbers. Never use a password for more than one account. Never store passwords on your computer.

3. Make sure any paper files are double locked when not under your direct surveillance. Never leave case files in your car, or on your desk.

4. Update your computer's operating system, web browsing programs, and other programs regularly (better yet, make sure they are all set to auto-update).

---

[9] http://www.ama-assn.org/ama/pub/physician-resources/solutions-managing-your-practice/coding-billing-insurance/hipaahealth-insurance-portability-accountability-act/hipaa-violations-enforcement.page

5. And finally, don't store client records any longer than you're required:
   5 years, 7 years, 12 years—whatever the rule is in your area, destroy
   old case files accordingly.

Good luck!

Lesson 40:
Electronic Health Records in Today's Private Counseling Practice

While some counselors today are reaching for their pens and notepads, others are reaching for their laptops (and iPads!). With the help of Electronic Health Record (EHR) and Practice Management (PM) software, counselors are trashing their metal filing cabinets and announcing that they're "going green!" Eco-friendship aside, a good EHR-PM program can help a practice to organize files, improve treatment planning, measure client sessions and attrition, monitor client balances and accounts relievable, track authorizations, file insurance claims, schedule appointments, and more...or at least that's what it says on the box!

The technological learning curve aside, counselors today face numerous roadblocks implementing EHR-PM software into their practices. This lesson will address those roadblocks, and share the experiences of several counselors' journey into the paperless.

Roadblock One: The Cost

"Go paperless and earn up to $44,000 in incentives." This is the sales pitch of many EHR software companies today. And it's true. In 2009, President Obama signed into law the Health Information Technology for Economic and Clinical Health Act (HITECH). Under HITECH, qualified providers can receive up to $44,000 in Medicare bonus incentives if they demonstrate the "meaningful use" of an EHR system.

But wait...did you catch that? Medicare. Counselors can't accept Medicare! In fact, even if they could, a "qualified provider" is a physician—not an LPC.

Unfortunately, the HITECH stimulus package doesn't account for mental health professionals trying to turn the electronic corner. Worse yet, the generous incentives have served to inflate the price of EHR programs across the board. This makes sense when considering that even if an EHR-PM software suite costs $50,000, a group practice of four MDs will still turn a 6-figure bonus for implementing the EHR-PM software.

Journey into the Paperless

Wendy Molinaroli, a counselor in Charleston SC, is no stranger to EHR. In fact, she's been looking for suitable software for her solo private practice since 2000, and has logged hundreds of hours in the search. One of her findings: most EHR-PM programs are priced too high for counselors. For example:

- **Amazing Charts:** $1999 per year for the first provider, $995 for each additional provider.
- **All Scripts:** $699 per month per doctoral-level provider, $474 for master's level.
- **Soapware:** $3000.00 per year, per provider.
- **Praxis:** $6995.00 per year for the first provider, $2995.00 for each additional provider.
- **AdvancedMD:** Nearly $1000 per month, per provider.

What's notable is that many programs aren't just expensive; the prices are incompatible with counseling practices of any size. Specifically, the rates are so high on a per-user basis, that even if a group counseling practice made *infinity dollars*, the practice still would not be able to afford the per-user cost because masters-level clinicians don't bill enough to justify a software fee of several hundred (or thousand) dollars a month (this is particularly true for practices that include part-time clinicians).

Roadblock Two: Software Problems

Fred Porter[10], owner of a New England psychiatry practice paid thousands to get started with his web based EHR-PM program. But when he loaded his patient list of several thousand into the system, it slowed to a crawl. Fred explains, "We would watch the appointment calendar load, one line of text at a time. It could take 10 minutes to check a patient in." In addition, there were state specific regulations for filing insurance claims that the out of state software vendor wasn't used to—so claims were getting denied. And so began a ritual for Fred, of finding bugs and calling the software company to try and get them fixed. Fred explains, "If you deal with a larger company like Siemens you won't have delays, and they have experience with practices nationwide; but a small practice can't afford that. So I'd call them and say 'this or that doesn't work' and they'd say they'd look into it—it felt to me like I was teaching the vendor." A month into his implementation, Fred received an unexpected bill in the mail for customer support! "I couldn't believe it— I'm helping them fix their software. But what are you going to do? Once you've committed to a program, had it installed, trained your staff—it's a nightmare to switch. They not only have all your data, all your insurance claims are in their software!"

It's hard to believe the lack of viable programs when an Internet search will turn up pages of results. In the last year, Wendy and I have both test-driven dozens of programs, sharing our notes (and disappointments) about each. Names have been removed to protect the guilty, but the problems are

---

[10] Name Changed

numerous, pervasive, and render many EHR-PM software options on the market unusable. Here are some of the problems we encountered:

- Help tickets go unanswered
- Software has downtime
- Software is cripplingly slow
- Broken features
- Basic features missing
- A difficult to use interface
- Billing claims sent improperly, or not at all
- Billing claims sent repeatedly (in error)
- Reports are faulty, or altogether unavailable.

Wendy explains, "Some software is okay on the notes [EHR] side, but the practice management and billing side is poor. Some software is the other way around. No one seems to have a complete usable package."

Making it Work

Ryan Neace, a Central VA based counselor, has gone paperless without the use of EHR software. In his practice, every therapy office is assigned its own iPad, on which is loaded a simple note-taking program called "smartNote," available in the iTunes app store, for $2.99. Ryan explains, "The client files are password protected. Besides that, the application couldn't be more basic. It can't run reports, such as sessions booked, and it has no billing capabilities whatsoever. The program works for us because we don't need much in the realm of reporting, and because we're a cash-only practice."

Counselor Wendy is on her fourth software suite in as many years. Her first software had "updating and synching" problems, the second company went out of business, the third software never ran properly (according to Wendy, "they blamed Bill Gates for their software being crappy"), and as for the fourth program, the note-taking side works well, but the PM side has so many serious billing problems that Wendy is being forced to switch software vendors again. Wendy laments, "Even after all my searching, I haven't found a single software program I could recommend to counselors!"

Fred has stuck it out with his software provider through what he describes as "a year and a half of struggles." The PM side of the software is working, but he has yet to begin using the EHR. Fred explains, "because the financials weren't working, I wasn't going to tie myself to the EHR. I'm already paying for it—I've just been reluctant to use it." He says he feels fortunate that his software developer 'got it' and was able to make adjustments to the software. He plans to begin using the EHR soon, and is excited about some other features, such as automated reminder calls. Fred says "Reminder calls keep the no show rates down to 5%, but it takes an enormous amount of resources for receptionists to manually make each call." As a final issue for Fred, even choosing a small EHR-PM vendor, one ad-on feature is still out of his budget. Fred says, "The electronic prescription writing is a bit expensive. It's $60 a month per provider. I have 12 prescribers, but some only work one day a week, so I can't justify the cost." Still, Fred is positive about the prognosis, saying, "We're getting there. Slower than I had hoped but we're getting there..."

As for my practice, we began using EHR-PM software in 2009. We thought that an EHR system would help us to better organize records, and would make records easier to retrieve when clients request them. As director, I also saw value in having a solution that combines note taking with insurance billing.

In choosing an EHR-PM platform, our team sorted through what features would be most helpful for our practice. We wanted to find a web-based program that didn't need installation on every office computer. This eliminated many options. Price eliminated others. Trying demo-versions of various suites eliminated even more, as many look like a flashback to DOS. In the end, we found a low cost program called "Office Ally" (Cost for EHR is $29.95, plus $15 per provider, per month. The PM software is basically free).

The team was excited about the program. However, once implementation began, the excitement waned. The software was not nearly as user friendly as we had hoped, and the learning curve was brutal. There is a lot of dialogue during the training process that sounds like: "you need to click here, then here, then click the drop down menu here, and ignore those sections there because those features don't apply to us."

Today, several years into our Office Ally subscription, our staff still dislikes it, as does our in-house billing department, who warns that the software will become decreasingly able to meet our needs as the practice grows. Also, it only works well on Internet Explorer, and it has regular bugs, crashes, and downtime.

In an attempt to phase out Office Ally, in 2011 we tested a new software program with a handful of staff. While the notes side worked well, the PM side was wrought with problems. We are now in the process of implementing a third software program. This time, the practice purchased a higher-priced solution, with hopes that it will lead to better outcomes. In the next year we will be spending north of $10,000 on EHR-PM software (we'll let you know how it goes).

Despite the troubles, overall EHR-PM software has helped the practice. Note taking has improved, as has the organization of client files. We can view a history of sessions at a glance, and how much has been paid to each clinician from insurance and co-pays. It's also a nice perk not to have a growing mountain of filing cabinets crowd the office.

No One's Missing the Boat

Sometimes it's not worth being an early adopter. As someone who has spent hundreds of hours searching for and testing EHR-PM programs, it's infuriating to know that at some point in the future—perhaps even soon—there will be a clear industry leader. Choosing software will be quick, easy, and maybe even affordable. So, if you feel like you're missing the boat on EHR–PM software, you're not. The boat isn't even in the water yet!

Lesson 41:
Shut Up and Do Your Work

My phone dings, whirs, beeps, buzzes. I don't even know which app is signaling to me at any given time; but it's constant. I mute them, but they turn themselves back on. At my business, there's always a crisis, always a critic, and always something vying for my attention. But the loudest noise of all by far; the only noise with any real power to distract me from my work is the one in my head.

When someone calls my phone, it only rings — pathetically. It has no other power to do anything. But, if undisciplined, the voice in my mind will yell, "Drop everything and answer that phone!" and then with a simple "hello" I'm on break from my work. Some research studies suggest that email, social media, and text messaging erodes the attention centers of our brains, decreasing our productivity. An entire industry has emerged with products to help us improve "focus" and "brainpower." I don't buy it.

> *"Barring any serious clinical diagnosis, our minds have all the attention capacity we need; we're just looking for an excuse to distract ourselves. Throughout the workday text messages are candy, and we're acting like children."*

> *"It sounds blunt, but this month I'm writing 5 ideas to help us shut up and do our work."*

1) Accept that All Resistance Comes from Within

"Resistance" is anything that prevents us from getting our work done, and these days it seems to come from every direction: our coworkers, news feeds,

702 Facebook friends, even our families. Steven Pressfield, in his book The War of Art, explains "Dad gets drunk, Mom gets sick, Janie shows up for church with an Oakland Raiders tattoo. It's more fun than a movie. And it works: Nobody gets a damn thing done."

While resistance seems to come from outside us, in truth is it a 100% self-generated toxin. It infects us when we attempt any act that makes us feel vulnerable, or that delays immediate gratification in favor of long-term growth or productivity. How difficult is resistance to overcome? Pressfield offers this hyperbole; "[Hitler] at eighteen ... moved to Vienna to live and study...Ever see one of his paintings? Neither have I. Resistance beat him. Call it overstatement but I'll say it anyway: it was easier for Hitler to start World War II than it was for him to face a blank square of canvas."

2) Force Yourself to Show Up Every day on Time.

When Earnest Hemmingway was interviewed about the challenge of writing, he said, "All you do is sit down at a typewriter and bleed." I used to agree with this—that writing was as draining as bleeding out. But it's not quite accurate. The hardest thing about writing, or going for a walk, or running a business is sitting down, standing up, or showing up (every day on time), respectively. The first keystroke, step, or executive action of the day is always the hardest. That's why most ultimate failures in business aren't the product of failed actions, but the failure to act. As counselors, we spend years telling ourselves "I'm going to start/grow/fix my practice; I'm just going to do it later." Later never comes. After years of stagnation, practices don't go up in flames—they quietly die.

Are you running your practice like it's a hobby? Those who do this never make the transition from 'amateur' to 'professional.'

> *"An amateur waits for 'inspiration to come' and lacks consistency. The amateur will never grow his business (or compose his symphony; or finish his novel). In contrast, for the professional, 'Inspiration strikes every morning at nine o'clock sharp.'"*

3) Don't Get Distracted, but Stay Focused on Your Path

A counseling practice can be focused on mediation, seminars, intensive outpatient programs, art therapy, equine therapy, counseling video games, etc.! There are many attractive paths to success and it's normal to have some 'buyer's remorse' as it applies to your practice's focus. However, once you choose a direction, unless there are real signals that you're on the wrong path, don't redirect! To make progress in any one direction you may need to ignore other opportunities. For example, Buffalo Wild Wings dropped weck sandwiches to focus on their now famous Buffalo wings (that's why some people still call it 'BW3s.' They were once "Buffalo Wild Wings and Weck"). Had they not focused their attention on wings, but tried to be the best at wings, weck, steak, and polish sausage, they never would have become a breakout success.

Often when we deviate from our focus it's because we're afraid of the failure we might face if we continue down our current road. It's resistance in another form! It looks a lot like work to start over, and there's a lot of activity to be sure, but it's just running back to the safety of square one. Consider this: Last year I spoke with a therapist who had a growing art therapy business. She had plans to expand it throughout her community. Recently, I asked her about her progress and she said, "We're putting art therapy on hold to launch our mediation program." That's Resistance!

4) Know that Meetings, Workshops, Collaboration can = Procrastination

Collaboration is imperative to the health of a company. However, resistance finds a way to pervert it.

Ever have a coworker who spends all day talking about his work? He writes an email, and then he reads you the email he just wrote! Or he makes a phone call and then recites the entire conversation to you line-by-line!? This person thinks he's working, but he's avoiding work with every new office conversation. Same goes for the person who wants to schedule a "follow-up meeting" when there's really nothing to meet about. Or the coworker who wants to "get some feedback" on something she's been working on for 32 minutes. Or perhaps the person who's signing up for a workshop (it should be called a "noworkshop"). It all looks a lot like work, doesn't it?

Sometimes what we pass off for work are emotional-support-seeking behaviors that let procrastination (i.e., resistance) overtake us.

5) Agree that Very Successful People
Overcome Very Difficult Odds

Need a good, justifiable, excuse not to work on your practice? Let me help.

Top Excuses:
- Nine out of 10 businesses fail
- You're stuck because you never learned business in school
- Growing a practice doesn't fit for you at this age

- You're working at your own pace
- The insurance companies are making it impossible
- You don't have the capital to 'do it right'
- You have medical issues
- You have some personal issues you need to 'take care of' first

It's not hard to find reasons not to work. I promise, no one will blame you. In fact, most people are doing the same thing. But just remember, successful people don't let adversity stop them: Tolstoy had thirteen kids and still wrote War and Peace. Oprah was brutalized as a child. Richard Branson has Dyslexia. Steven King's first novel was rejected 30 times.

Are your challenges greater than theirs? No? Then let's shut up and do our work.

Lesson 42:
Productivity: Turn Off Your Phone

Detach for Better Clarity

"To grow your business, you need to stop working 'in' it and spend more time working 'on' it."

Some months ago, I wrote an article about the importance of rest, and shutting down your phone was one step in that process. This month, as I talk about the importance of turning off your phone again, I'm not suggesting taking another break. It may seem like a paradox, but unplugging from your business might be just what you need to grow that business.

Here's the typical day for many small business owners: The bookkeeper calls with questions about your monthly P&L. An unhappy customer emails a complaint. Your attorney needs documents. Google sends you a notice that your website isn't "mobile compliant." These are important issues, and there are serious consequences if they go ignored, so you respond to one, after another, after another.

You feel productive and you're resolving the issues fairly well, but there's still a problem. Each of the tasks above is you working "in" your business. To grow your business, you need to stop working "in" it and spend more time working "on" it.

It has never been harder than it is today to work "on" one's business. Many of

us are never more than a few feet from our cell phones at any given time ...
ever.

And the word is out. When someone sends an email or a text, they expect a
response immediately, because they know you saw it! Worse yet, you may
feel a compulsion to meet that expectation. Simply put, many of us are too
accessible, and the never-ending stream of emails and phone calls keep us
firmly planted "in" our businesses.

Here's how to break out.

1. Turn off your Phone, and Log Out of your Email

As I'm writing this column, I've shut down my cell phone, I've logged out of
my email and I've hid myself in a therapy room where no one can find me.
Mid-workday, sometimes it's the only way I can escape both physically and
mentally from the daily goings-on.

In addition, every night around 5 p.m. I shut down my phone. It stays off until
8:30 the next morning. Am I on break after 5 p.m.? I wish. That's when I can
focus exclusively on projects and ideas that can move the business forward.
I'll do it during the day too — as much as I can — but during evenings and
weekends, I'm definitely not getting pulled "in" to my business.

After shutting down my phone, for music and web searches I'll use an old
iPhone 4 with no cell service and no email app installed. If I need to do
serious online research, I'll grab my iPad (the one my daughter claims is her
iPad), or I'll use my computer and make sure I'm logged out of email.

Do I miss personal calls? Yes. But again, this process isn't about rest or recreation. It's about working "on" your business. If I wanted personal calls, I'd activate the iPhone. As it is, my closest friends, family and even some team members (in the instance of an emergency) can call my wife's phone if they need to track me down.

2. Climb "Out" of Your Business

If you're building a business, there will ALWAYS be ongoing problems: An ex-employee is extorting you. A customer is threatening you. An insurance company is auditing you.

Turning your phone off is a start, but you need some mental space too if you're going to get creative and work "on" your business. Drinking Scotch works for mental space, but hurts productivity. Without chemical help, it will take time to clear your head. With that said, a good business book or turning your attention to some project that really excites you will help you mentally climb "out" of your business more quickly.

When done right, time working "on" your business will advance you forward. For example:

1. You read the book "Be our Guest" by the Disney Institute, and you jot down pages of ideas for improving your company's customer service
2. You design and test a paperless intake and informed consent process
3. You plot out where your next office is going to be — and determine when you will be able to open. That's working "on" the business.

3. Climbing Back "In"

If you're clamoring to turn your phone back on, or check your email, you haven't had it off long enough.

When done right, the mental space and general feeling that comes from working "on" your business will make you reluctant to turn back to the daily minutia. You won't want to be pulled back "in." Hold on to this perspective. The more time you can find where you don't need to work "in" your business, the more success you'll have growing your business.

With that said, as you cycle your phone on and the beeps of missed texts, emails and voicemails come streaming in, that clear mental space you've achieved will help you handle the day's challenges even better.

Lesson 43:
Stress Management and Rest for the Entrepreneur

The Entrepreneur's Nerves are not Made of Steel

Building and sustaining a business is a day-in, day-out war between uncertainty and perseverance. Make few bad decisions or take your "eye off the ball" for just a minute, and it could be "game over." As an entrepreneur, your ability to persist through prolonged times of risk and stress is as important to your company's survival as it is your own.

Says one entrepreneur: "*Running your own business takes nerves of steel.*" The trouble is that nerves aren't steel, they're nerves — and they can be broken. For many, the long hours and the stress of entrepreneurship have their costs.

Last month, a friend and colleague called me to say that his wife brought him to the emergency room after he experienced several days of heart palpitations. The diagnosis wasn't a heart attack but high blood pressure brought on by stress. He was prescribed an SSRI (and is doing better). Others in his shoes are handling stress by self-medicating with alcohol, marijuana, or carrying a bottle of trusty benzodiazepines in their pockets.

Most of my columns are about lighting a fire and encouraging the hard work of entrepreneurship. This month we're going flip the coin and talk about stress management and life balance. There's a lot of advice available on the topic already, but here are a few strategies I've found to be particularly effective for the entrepreneur.

Sleep

Everyone's heard about the importance of sleep. But too often we think, "That's for the guy (or gal) who's NOT trying to build a business." Not true. Sleep is particularly important for entrepreneurs. When you're tired, your ability to manage stress drops through the floor, and you don't think clearly or creatively. In sum, you make terrible business decisions.

While the effects of sleep deprivation are harsh, the benefits of sleep are impressive. One Stanford University study found that basketball players who slept about 10 hours a night sprinted faster and demonstrated a 9% increase in free throw and 3-point shooting accuracy.

While a typical recommendation is 7 to 9 hours per night, different persons need different amounts of sleep. To determine how much you likely need, ask yourself, "*How much would I sleep if I didn't have to work?*" Try sleeping that much.

Exercise

Exercise is important for the entrepreneur. Studies have shown that moderate exercise improves mood and creativity. If you're new to exercise, try scheduling just 30 minutes of gym time into your daily routine. Be prepared that there will be days when it seems that just 30 minutes is going to rob too much time from your mounting workload. And there will be some days when you're so mentally pre-occupied with work that you just won't be able to convince yourself to go. If you need to skip a day—so be it, just don't skip a week!

On days when I'm crunched for time, I can still walk for an hour without losing any work time because there are always business calls that I can make while walking (also, I can sometimes find solutions to business problems faster during a walk).

Of course, if the idea of incorporating exercise into your daily routine makes you tired, first focus on getting more sleep.

Side Note: At my company, we've experimented with what we thought would be an effective work-exercise hybrid — treadmill desks. We found that it's really difficult to get work done when on a treadmill desk: Graphic design is impossible. It's difficult to focus when answering even simple emails. However, standing desks seem to work well as long as there's also an option for a person to sit if he/she gets tired.

Create a Work-free Zone

There was a time that I would maximize my home for productivity. I built a home office, even though I had an office at work. Like many entrepreneurs, I told myself that having a home office would make my life easier (and more productive). I could be home more with family. I could get work done in the mornings, even before getting dressed. And I could work in the evenings. And the weekends (woo-hoo)! What a terrible idea. Doing work at home — in the proximity of family — is not the same as being home with family.

I've since turned my home office into a mini home theatre. Instead of having a dedicated space to work at home, I now have a dedicated space at home to not work. I still work at home, but my house no is longer a trigger to keep working.

Schedule Fun

As an entrepreneur, you have a vast amount of work to complete at any given time, so you train yourself on being productive every spare moment. While others are standing in line, you're checking on the status of your new office. When others are listening to music while driving, you're on a conference call. It's a skill you've developed over time and it helps you keep ahead.

The dark side of this ability is that you've trained yourself — if there's any gap in your schedule — to default to working. Because of this, if you don't schedule your fun you'll end up updating your website on Saturday nights, and sending business emails on Sunday mornings.

It might sound "un-spontaneous" or "not fun" to schedule recreation (common criticisms), but if you want to make sure your take a break — you better book that time. Also, there's something therapeutic about having a packed daytime business itinerary and also a scheduled dinner with friends at the end of it.

No Guilt

Finally, let yourself off the hook a little. You are your most valuable resource, and like any other resource you need downtime and maintenance. Playing video games or reading gossip magazines, or whatever it is that you find frivolous or fun, is an important part of being productive.

These a few strategies I've found helpful for managing stress and finding balance. Strategies others (not me) have found helpful: yoga, meditation, specific diets, time in nature, music, limiting use of electronics, and there are many others. What stress-reducing techniques work for you?

401: Selling a Counseling Practice

Lesson 44:
Cashing in: How to Sell a Counseling Private Practice

Valuing Your Practice

Interested in selling your counseling therapy practice? We pay top dollar for excellent counseling businesses. Call Dr. Anthony Centore directly at **617-513-5433**.

If you're just getting started in private practice, selling your counseling business is possibly the last thing on your mind. However, it's never too early to start laying the groundwork for building a counseling practice that will someday be attractive to an acquirer. In fact, realizing at the beginning that there will one day be an ending is good forethought.

There are lots of reasons someone might decide to sell their practice. Consider:

- Might you decide to relocate at some point during your career?
- Might you ever want to change careers?
- When do you hope to retire? Do you plan to work in private practice until you're as old as Irvin Yalom (80)?

Think that you're too young to contemplate an exit strategy? Try this: A recent Stanford University study suggests that looking at an age-enhanced picture of yourself will motivate you to save more for retirement. That being said, counselors today, as a rule, are already in the second half of their careers. Of the AAMFT's 25,000+ members, the mean age is 55. Also, this year, more than one fourth of attendees at the ACA national conference were 56 or older.

As counselors consider retirement, some are finding that the practices they've built for much of their careers have little market value, or few interested acquirers. Hence, instead of selling their companies for a tidy sum, counselors are simply rolling them up—locking the doors, shuttering the windows, switching off the lights, and disconnecting the phones. This sounds harsh. A counselor might say, "After decades of work, do I have nothing to show for it?" The answer, "Of course not. Your practice has provided you a good living, rewarding work, and you've helped a lot of clients. It's just that what you've created doesn't have value that can be transferred to another business owner."

How to Value your Company:

There are many formulas for valuing companies. For service businesses, one popular method is to calculate a multiple of revenue. Depending on the industry, a services firm can be worth between one and two times revenue. Businesses can also be valued based on their EBITDA, an acronym that stands for Earnings Before the deduction of Interest, Tax, Depreciation, and Amortization (to keep it simple, let's just say "yearly profit"). A firm may be worth as much as two to three times EBITDA. While these numbers provide a starting point, they are also flawed for determining a business's exact worth. According to one expert "The problem is that these formulas are almost always too simplistic to serve as anything more than a very rough guide for the sale of real businesses."

Your company could be worth a lot more, or a lot less, than the formula above might suggest. For instance, say you have contracts guaranteed to earn your company revenue for the next 5 years (a court contract to counsel DUI offenders, for instance). Or, say that the sale of your business includes material assets—a slew of new high-end equipment, or even a building. Either of these scenarios could raise the value of your business.

However, your company could be worth less than the formulaic value. For example, say that your company's revenue or profit has been declining for the last several years. This downward trend would be a red flag to potential acquirers.

Second, say that the owner is also the company's manager, but she doesn't take a salary. In this case, the company could show a profit of $85,000. However, when one adjusts for a manager's salary, the business is only breaking even. In this instance, acquirer isn't buying a business; he or she is buying a job.

Third, the value of a company could be less if the company's key revenue producer will be leaving after the sale. This happens often in the counseling field. A company for sale will show gross revenues of $250,000. However, $150,000 of that revenue is a product of the owner's counseling fees. Once the owner sells and departs, the company will stop producing most of its revenue.

A thought to consider as you evaluate you company's price: "If I leave the practice, what remains that an acquirer would consider valuable?" The answer to this question is not always obvious. A dedicated staff is valuable. A telephone number that generates several appointments a day is valuable. The billing system, email lists, website, relationships with insurance companies—all these things could represent an opportunity for an acquirer.

Common Mistakes in Valuing a Business:

You love your practice. You've put your heart and soul into it, and to you its value is significant—any acquirer would be lucky to have it! Trust me, I understand. But a prospective buyer is looking at your business without emotion. Their offer will be based on the financial opportunity your company presents. Here are two common mistakes a business owner can make when valuing his or her company:

Valuing for Growth Potential

Too often a business owner will value his or her company not based on revenues and profits, but on what he or she believes the company is capable of earning in the future. Below is a real example of a counseling practice making this mistake. The owner is trying to sell the business on the "great opportunity" available for a buyer to grow the practice.

> *"Potential co-operative marketing with other health related professionals in same location. [A new owner can also] Expand professional referral network. [A new owner also has the] Potential to expand hours/days of operation or add complementary services. [New owner could also] Leverage social media marketing for targeted local advertising."*

What an opportunity! Sure, an acquirer can work harder than the last owner, and grow the company. That's a given. But a seller can't value their company on potential growth. As a note, if the seller is convinced such opportunities are low hanging fruit, it's wise for the seller to capitalize on those growth opportunities *before* selling the business! Not only will the seller make more money prior to the sale, he or she could command a higher purchase price.

Buyers are looking for businesses with predictable revenues, not a lottery ticket. They will value an acquisition based on what they are actually getting.

The Value of Reputation:

A seller might say, "We're very respected in the community. This makes us more valuable than one times revenue." Not exactly. While having a poor reputation could lower your practice's value, being "respected in the community" is the expectation, not the exception. Hence, while a great reputation may not translate into a larger than usual purchase price, a great reputation does make your company more sellable. Presumably, your reputation has also helped you to grow revenues, which *will* command your purchase price!

Letting Go:

When selling your practice, be ready to let go. After the sale, your practice might change in many ways: The logo. The name. The location. The specialization. And the list goes on...

I recently had several weeks of correspondence with a woman who had advertised the sale of her sex therapy practice. After talking with her at length, and making several proposals for the sale of her practice, she flatly turned me down. No counter offer. Just, "No thank you." I asked her,

Have I offended you?

No! You have been very polite.

Have I been pushy?

No! You have been extremely patient.

Is it an issue of money?

No! Your price seems fair to me.

Has another buyer expressed interest?

No! There are no other interested parties.

"Then what!?" I asked. She told me that she decided that she only wanted to sell her practice to another sex therapist. I tried to explain, "I plan to hire a sex therapist to be a key member of the team."

"That's the other thing," she said. "I've been a solo practice for 20 years. I don't like the idea of a larger practice taking over."

And that was it. She left our negotiation to find a solo sex therapist practitioner she could train to run her practice for the next 20 years, as she's run it for the last 20 years. To her, the thought of her practice changing was sacrilege.

I hope she finds the buyer she is looking for, as she had been winding down her operations, and is now only open 4 days a week. Also, being in her 70s, she hopes to pursue new activities with her husband while she still has the enough health to do so. Frankly, if she doesn't find the perfect buyer soon, like so many others, she will find herself turning off her lights, and disconnecting her phone.

A buyer can respect and honor the seller's legacy. A buyer can show the seller how much he/she will care for their clients and community. However, few buyers are willing to do things exactly like the seller! At some point, sellers need to let go.

Prelude to Part Two:

The topic of creating a sellable practice is a big one—an entire book on the topic would still be just a cursory overview. Hence, you've just read part one of a two-part column. Stay tuned until next month, when I will be presenting "11 Ways to Increase the Value of Your Counseling Practice."

11 Ways to Increase the Value of Your Counseling Practice

Are you thinking about selling your counseling business? Thriveworks will pay top dollar for counseling / therapy practices with great reputations. Call Dr. Anthony Centore directly at **617-513-5433.**

In the previous column, we discussed the importance of building a sellable private practice, and we looked at formulas for valuing a service business. In this column, we'll review 11 ways that you can make your business worth top dollar to an acquirer.

1. Brand

In the counseling industry, many practices are named after the owner, as in

"Amy Smith Counseling" or "Smith and Associates." This type of name could make transferring the business to an acquirer tricky.

Once upon a time, psychologist Dr. Wagner purchased a psychological testing practice called "Powell Associates" from a Dr. Powell. Dr. Wagner added his name, changing the business to "Powell and Wagner Associates." Today, if the practice is resold, what happens? Will it become "Powell, Wagner, and Smith Associates" even though Dr. Powell hasn't been with the company for over 20 years?

A personal brand runs the risk of communicating to customers that the value of a company resides in the founder—not the business' mission, product, service, or team. However, this seems to become less the case the larger and older a business is.

For instance, no one walks into a Walgreen's and demands to speak with Mr. Walgreen. No one goes to Ruth's Chris and expects their steak to be grilled by Chris, or Ruth (by the way, the restaurant got it's name when Ruth Fertel bought Chris Steak House). As for Dr. Wagner, he explains, "Someone might call and say 'My Grandfather used to see Dr. Powell.' They don't expect him to be here, but they still trust the brand."

While not insurmountable, life is a little easier for an acquirer when the founder's name is not inextricably tied to a practice. If you want to build a practice to sell, consider a brand name other than your own.

2. Beyond a Solo Practice

Solo-practices are often worth less than group practices. For this, there are two reasons. First, simply based on their size, solo-practices often produce lower revenues than group practices. Second, with a solo-practice, the business owner is the lead clinician. Hence, when the owner sells (and leaves the practice), the business stops generating revenue. A new owner has the daunting task of finding a new clinician, and building his/her caseload. In contrast, a group practice with several clinicians will continue generating revenue even when the original owner departs.

3. Consider an Earn Out

An "earn out" is when a seller accepts an offer for his/her company that is contingent on the company achieving specific financial goals over a period of time.

For example, a company might receive a purchase offer of $200,000. However, a percentage of the purchase price is contingent on the company earning their anticipated revenues the next three years.

If you are confident that your company is stable or growing, and if you're willing to stay involved in the management of your business for a while, accepting an earn out could help you to receive top dollar for your business.

4. Finance the Buyer

Many businesses are purchased in installments (this is also called "financing the buyer"). In an installment sale, sellers receive a portion of their purchase price up front, and then the remainder is paid in installments (perhaps over 3 years).

There are some perks to an installment sale, for sellers. First, a seller can charge interest (often 5-10%) on the outstanding balance. Also, with and installment sale, the seller can include a "claw back" provision in the sale agreement, which means that if the buyer defaults on payments, the seller can repossess their business and resell it to a new buyer.

5. Focus on New Clients, not Existing Caseloads

Current caseloads are worth less than new client inquiries. For example, one practice for sale has four clinicians, each with full caseloads of long-term clients. The practice receives 20 new client inquiries per month. In contrast, another practice for sale has only two full-time clinicians, and 100 new client inquiries per month.

While the former practice is generating higher revenues, it also places a buyer at higher risk. At only 20 inquiries per month, the business won't recover in the event of clinician turnover, as the practice is not generating enough leads to build a new counselor's caseload. Hence, even though the second practice serves fewer clients, it could be more valuable than its counterpart.

Tip: Having a rigorous system in place to document the volume of incoming inquiries from various sources (email, website, yellow pages ads, etc.), and what portion of them become new patients, will increase the value of your practice to certain buyers.

6. Credentialing

In many markets today, accepting clients' health insurance is important to a counseling business' success and stability. Hence, it is increasingly important to buyers to find a practice that is credentialed with insurance companies.

A business seller should make sure that their insurance credentialing is such that it will transfer to an acquirer. When possible, a practice should have group contracts with insurance companies, as well as individual provider contracts.

7. A Committed, Compatible Staff

Sometimes, when a practice is sold, staff doesn't survive the transition. Here are two real-life instances wherein existing staffs were incompatible with new management.

- A psychiatry practice is being purchased from an absentee owner/manager. A few weeks before the close of the sale, the new owner begins working in the practice and begins to implement some basic rules of operation for the administrative staff. They revolt! The staff destroys documents, cancels appointments, refuses to answer the phone, and creates a hostile work environment (they were also, as it was later discovered, stealing from the company). The new owner has no choice but to fire the staff, and hire a new administrative team.

- A buyer of a counseling practice discovers that the previous owner has overpaid his clinicians by compensating them heavily for completing basic administrative tasks the previous owner did not want to do. The new owner realizes that the practice cannot survive without the clinicians forgoing their administrative duties (along with the extra income). The counselors do not respond well to receiving what they perceive as "a cut in pay", and several leave the practice. Revenues drop by over 40%, and the practice doesn't recover for over a year.

In both these instances, the owners had little choice but to start over with new staff. However, a buyer will almost always want an existing team to stay. Hence, anything that commits employees to the business, such as a "long term incentive plan" (a bonus accrued and paid on a rolling basis over years of service) could be valuable to a buyer, as it helps to improve staff retention.

8. Quality Hard Assets

To the extent that a buyer can utilize them, hard assets have value. Recently, I visited a counseling practice for sale in New England. The owner valued her furnishings (chairs, desks, computer equipment, etc.) at $12,000. However, almost everything in her offices was tired, old, and generally below our standard of quality. Hence, to us her "furnishings" would have to be replaced entirely and therefore had zero value. In contrast, if we visited a practice with therapy offices that were "move in ready," such assets would be worth top dollar, as we wouldn't need to put out the cost (and effort) of furnishing the space.

9. Lease

If your practice rents space, the lease your business holds can affect the sale. Buyers always want low rent guaranteed for multiple years, as well as the flexibility to cut and run anytime. This, of course, is unlikely! As a seller, you are in good shape with a fair lease, with some amount of security for the buyer. Avoid these three bad lease situations:

- The practice has a 5-year lease in a bad location. The buyer would prefer to move the office, but breaking the lease will be too expensive.
- The lease is non-transferable, and the landlord wants a 20% rent increase from any new tenant/owner.
- The lease terminates within a year, and the landlord plans to raise the rent more than 4%.

10. Be Honest and Open

As part of our growth strategy, my company has started looking for counseling practices to purchase. We talk with many providers who have listed their businesses for sale. At times, even after we sign a confidentiality agreement, some are reluctant to talk openly about their practices' weaknesses (owners never have a problem talking about their strengths). This evasiveness often ruins the potential for a sale.

Sometimes owners will overestimate the size of their practice. I recently met with an owner who claimed that her practice was scheduling 5-10 new clients per week.

However, when we looked at her practice's record of first sessions, it was actually scheduling 6-12 new clients...per month! That's a forth of what the seller reported! Either this seller had did not understand her business, or she was trying to mislead.

Misrepresenting one's company to a potential buyer will slow down the acquisition process, and could result in future legal action from a buyer. So be honest! No business is perfect, and a serious buyer isn't looking for perfection.

11. Finish Strong

Many practices are for sale by clinicians who are nearing retirement. This is a great reason to sell! However, clinicians commonly make the same mistake. That is, they begin winding down their practices while (or before) their companies are put up for sale. For example, a counselor who once saw 30 clients a week, while trying to sell her practice, might decrease her caseload to 20. This ill-timed decrease lowers revenues, and increases the risk for potential buyers, who will need to try and rejuvenate a shrinking practice.

My father once told me, "When painting, stop while you still have about 20% of your energy left." His reasoning, "You'll need energy to rinse out your brushes, and clean up the room." It's good advice. Similarly, counselors are much better off selling their practices while they still have energy to finish strong. To attract good buyers and to earn top dollar, make sure your numbers are stable, even trending upward!

Lesson 45:
5 More Tips for Building a Sellable Practice

Selling a practice. It might be the largest single financial transaction of your life. And it could go very well, or it might not happen at all. Depending on the choices you make, your practice could fund your retirement...*or it might be worth close to nothing.* While it's a much larger topic than this column can do justice, this month I'll provide a few tips to help you increase the value of your counseling practice.

A stable, dedicated team

Click "Meet the team" on the website of any practice and you'll probably see a webpage that can't keep up with all the staff changes. Bios and pictures rarely reflect who's actually on board (team photos are the worst, they're *never* accurate). In many practices, while a few core providers are longstanding, most depart in less than 2 years. The tenure of your staff is important because an acquirer will approach the purchase of your practice asking him/herself "How many of these staff are going to survive the acquisition process? How many are likely to quit in the next year—*or even set up competing offices*?" In our field, there's no inventory, there are no patents. The value of your business is closely tied to your team. If you can find a way to develop a clinical team that's onboard to stay, you will fetch a higher price for your practice.

Key person discount

Whenever a small business is for sale, an acquirer wants to know if it's self-sustaining, or if it only works because of a talented owner-manager. An acquirer doesn't want the task of replacing the heart of the practice after the current owner departs, and he/she will lower their offer if that's the case. This is such an important issue, persons experienced with mergers and acquisitions have a name for it—the key person (or "key man") discount. Hence, the more you aren't a "key person" necessary for day-to-day operations the better.

Growth

There's an old adage "If you're not growing you're dying" and basically it's a false platitude. However, showing year-after-year revenue growth—even slow growth—demonstrates to an acquirer that your practice is headed in the right direction. Contrarily, practices that are financially up and down show instability (and practices with declining revenues are a red flag).

As a side, my father used to say "*Quit painting when you're 80% tired. You'll need the last 20% for the cleanup.*" Think about this when timing the sale of your practice. Too often owners decide to sell only after they've begun "winding down." Don't do this! Sell when you still have passion and energy for your practice. Your last year should be your highest revenue (and hopefully most profitable) year.

Be a Strategic investment

A common misconception among sellers is that an acquirer will buy their business and grow the seller's brand. In truth, a buyer is usually already working in the industry and is more interested in building his/her *own* brand, and a smart strategic acquirer is asking her/himself the question "how will acquiring this company help me to sell more of *my* stuff?"

To be most valuable, have a practice that helps an acquirer to sell more of his/her own stuff. For example, if your practice provides something unique—say forensic consulting—this makes your practice more valuable than if you just did counseling appointments. Why? Because it's likely the acquirer doesn't have forensic consulting in his/her practice(s), but by learning your processes the acquirer learns how to add such offerings to his/her existing practice(s).

Show a Trajectory

You want to show an acquirer that your practice has a future, not just a track record. An example of the later is a longstanding practice that has consistent referrals coming in, but doesn't have any current marketing program (maybe it doesn't even have a website!). All the networking was done 20 years ago, and now the practice just gets referrals from those who've always given referrals. Why is this bad? Because it's voodoo! An acquirer doesn't know what to do with that—doesn't know how to grow or sustain it, and doesn't know when the magic will end. For all the acquirer knows, the people referring might be 6 seconds from retirement, or there might be a competitor slowly chipping away at that book of referral business.

501: Online Counseling – A Primer

Lesson 46:
Clinical Advantages and Disadvantages of Online Counseling

Raul is a Hispanic American looking for a counselor who speaks Spanish, and who understands first-hand his cultural perspectives. There's no one like this within 50 miles.

Dave can never seem to make his appointments. Because of no-shows, he's been "blackballed" from two dentists and one counselor already.

After an hour, Judy feels she's just beginning to get to the heart of what she needs to say—then the session ends. The last counselor Jamie saw made a pass at her. She vows never to put herself into that situation again. Ken has always felt that he doesn't articulate himself well verbally. However, he expresses himself quite well in writing. Jordan works 9 to 5, Monday through Friday, the same hours the counseling center is open. "People in therapy must not have jobs," she thinks to herself.

Brian is so ashamed he could never look a counselor in the eye. John lives in a small town. Not only does he not want his neighbors to know he's been having panic attacks, the only counselor is his daughter in-law.

Sayward is a Licensed Professional Counselor with medical conditions that make her unable to leave home. She wishes there was a way she could still use her 20-plus years of clinical experience.

* * *

These persons come from different walks of life. They have different stories. They struggle with dissimilar circumstances. But they have one thing in common—they all could be excellent candidates for Online Counseling.

Did you know that only 10% of depressed people who are referred by a physician to seek mental health services ever receive those services? Why is this? Is it because they do not want to get well, or are there other factors? As you might guess, the reasons are many; and include the problem that acquiring counseling is too difficult. Consider this, a man suffering from depression, to receive counseling must:

1. Overcome his apprehension, embarrassment and fear of seeking counseling
2. Come to terms that people in his community might find out he is in therapy
3. Research and locate reputable local counseling services
4. Make contact with a service (usually by phone) to schedule a session
5. Accept, if insurance is to be used, that he will be diagnosed with a psychological disorder that will go in his health record
6. Maintain motivation and courage while waiting for a scheduled session—the wait is often weeks or longer
7. Execute his intentions of arriving at the counseling appointment (which may necessitate taking time off work)

For a person battling even the most common life-issues, this is quite a series of tasks! And what is more, we—as counselors—cannot do much to make it easier. We often have long waiting lists for new clients, business hours that conflict with client work schedules; we allow clients to suffer social stigma, require them to travel to an unfamiliar place, and to arrive promptly and presentably; all while battling depression, anxiety, agoraphobia, grief, psychosis, or perhaps the greatest personal crisis of their life.

And all the while we wonder, "why is the compliance rate only 10%?"

In response to these tasks that reduce compliance so remarkably, several thousand counselors across the country are taking on the challenge of providing Online Counseling. They are using distance communication technologies like telephone, email, online text chat, and even videoconference. To these persons, Online Counseling is more than a back-up service for clients who just "can't make it in" for therapy (see table 1). Practitioners and researchers contend that, in numerous ways, Online Counseling can be ***superior*** to in-person counseling. These proposed advantages include a series of client-related factors presented below.

Proposed Advantages

Safety and Assertiveness

Online Counseling may increase clients' sense of safety, for they are able to receive help from within their home environment. This may help clients express themselves more fully.[11] For example, a study investigating Thai women in a co-ed online discussion found that females who took a passive role in face-to-face (FTF) interactions spoke more assertively and frequently

---

[11] Rosenfield, M. (2003). Telephone counselling and psychotherapy in practice. In S. Goss, K. Anthony (Eds.), *Technology in counseling and psychotherapy: A practitioner's guide* (pp. 93-108), Great Britain: Palgrave Macmillan; Suler, J. (2004). The psychology of text relationships, In R. Kraus, J. Zack, G. Strickler (Eds.). *Online counseling: A handbook for mental health professionals,* USA: Elsevier Academic Press.

online.[12]

Anonymity

While some counseling ethics codes regard client identification as necessary,[13] Online Counseling may still benefit from anonymity. For example, although a client may be required to provide their name and location, the Internet is a phenomenon where persons "communicate without the distractions of race, gender, age, size, or physical deformity or impairment."[14] One of the first online counseling services, called "Dear Uncle Ezra", was developed in 1986 by Cornell University.[15] This service allows queries from anonymous students, and a counselor responds via a public internet post. After 21 years this program is still active and users confirm that if it were not for the anonymous format, their problem issues would never have been revealed.

Social Stigma

Online Counseling assures clients they will not encounter their counselor in public[16], nor will they risk meeting persons from the community in the counselor's waiting room. Therefore, Online Counseling may be effective in

---

[12] Panyametheekul, S., & Herring, S. (2003, November). Gender and turn allocation in a Thai chat room. *Journal of Computer Mediated Communication, 9*(1).

[13] American Counseling Association Governing Council. (1999, October). *American Counseling Association code of ethics*. Author.

[14] Worona, S. (2003). Privacy, security, and anonymity: An evolving balance. *Educause Review, 38*(3), 62-63

[15] see http://ezra.cornell.edu

[16] Umefjord, G., Petersson, G., & Hamberg, K. (2003). Reasons for consulting a doctor on the internet: Web survey of users of an ask the doctor service. *Journal of Medical Internet Research, 5*(4):e26. Retrieved October 1, 2005, from http://www.jmir.org/2003/4/e26/

eliminating the social stigma of receiving therapy. One study investigating the use of phone counseling services by Arab Israeli callers found the stigma-free medium "may be a culturally appropriate modality of providing helping services to people who conventionally underutilize other forms of professional mental health intervention."[17] With similar ideas, the University of Wisconsin's counseling center allows therapists to be contacted by email, and George Mason University provides counseling by videoconference.[18]

Selection

Online Counseling may provide clients a greater selection of therapists to choose from. This is especially beneficial for persons looking for a counselor with specific experience, or with particular language, religious or ethnic understandings. Similarly, online support groups and forums dedicated to a variety of emotional problems have been present since the 1980's, and they have allowed persons to reach others dealing similar issues from across the world.[19]

---

[17] Al-Krenawi, A., Graham, J. R., & Fakher-Aldin, M. (2003, October). Telephone counseling: A comparison of Arab and Jewish Israeli usage. *International Social Work, 46*, 495.

[18] Carlson, S. (2002, November). As campus psychologists go online, they reach more students, and may also risk lawsuits. *Virtual Counseling, 49*(12), Retrieved April 01, 2006 from http://chronicle.com/free/v49/i12/12a03501.htm

[19] Carlson, S. (2002, November). As campus psychologists go online, they reach more students, and may also risk lawsuits. *Virtual Counseling, 49*(12), Retrieved April 01, 2006 from http://chronicle.com/free/v49/i12/12a03501.htm; Anthony, K. (2003). The use and role of technology in counselling and psychotherapy. In S. Goss, K. Anthony (Eds.), *Technology in counseling and psychotherapy: A practitioner's guide*, Great Britain: Palgrave Macmillan.

Accessibility

Online Counseling is advantageous to individuals residing in areas where counseling services are not available and with clients who are unable to leave home.[20] Also, while in-person counseling may be incompatible with a client's work schedule, Online Counseling possesses potential for 24 hour service availability—this is apparent with some crisis and Online Counseling services currently available 24 hours-a-day.

Even if counselors are not online or at a phone at all hours, counseling by email creates the perception of a counselor's perpetual availability. A client can communicate anytime, instead of waiting for a weekly or bi-weekly session. And since sessions do not have a defined beginning or end, a more intense psychological holding environment may be present between counselor-client exchanges.[21]

Affordability

Online Counseling may be more economical than in-person counseling due to lower overhead costs of counselors who do not need to rent commercial space, and the elimination of client and counselor commuting expenses. Concerning the value of time, the hours invested in counseling may be less with Online Counseling due to elimination of travel, lack of a waiting room, and the goal-directed dialog that often ensues with distance communication.

---

[20] Umefjord, G., Petersson, G., & Hamberg, K. (2003). Reasons for consulting a doctor on the internet: Web survey of users of an ask the doctor service. *Journal of Medical Internet Research, 5*(4):e26. Retrieved October 1, 2005, from http://www.jmir.org/2003/4/e26/ ;Rosenfield, 2003; ; Speyer, S. & Zack, J. (2003). *Online counselling: Beyond the pros and cons. Psychological, 23*(2), 11-14.

[21] Childress C. A. (2000). Ethical issues in providing online psychotherapeutic interventions. *Journal of Medical Internet Research, 2*(1): e5. Retrieved February 20, 2005, from http://www.jmir.org/2000/1/e5/

Regarding the latter, studies show that when communicating through phone and internet, "small talk" is greatly lessened and individuals address important issues faster.[22]

Proposed Disadvantages

In contrast, opponents of Online Counseling present these issues of concern—whether Online Counseling is ethical and legal, clinically effective, and financially viable.

Ethical and Legal Concerns

Similar to FTF provision, there are numerous ethical and legal issues in Online Counseling. Areas of particular concern include confidentiality, dealing with suicidal or dangerous clients, crisis response, and counseling clients across state lines.[23] While the latter is an issue most state boards have no formal position or legal precedent, a number of articles have been published concerning the ethical issues of Online Counseling, and they are commonly found to be challenging—but not impossible to resolve.

Rapport

Traditional views contend online communication (text-based) is an inferior

---

[22] Rosenfield, M. (1997). *Counselling by telephone.* London: Sage; Tidwell, L. C., & Walther, J. B. (2002). Computer-mediated communication effects on disclosure, impressions, and interpersonal evaluations: Getting to know one another a bit at a time. *Human Communication Research, 28,* 317-348.

[23] Kraus, R. (2004). Ethical and legal considerations for providers of mental health services online, In R. Kraus, J. Zack, G. Strickler (Eds.). *Online counseling: A handbook for mental health professionals,* USA: Elsevier Academic Press.

modality for developing rapport, due to the inability to read body language and hear emotional cues.[24] However, other empirical studies have found Online Counseling technologies to be effective rapport building mediums.[25] Today, the debate of how well rapport builds through distance communication continues.

Clinical Efficacy

According to ethical standards of the ACA, NBCC, and others, counselors are ethically obligated to provide viable treatment. With Online Counseling, while some studies contend efficacy to be inferior to in-person sessions,[26] others have found client improvement with various online and telephone

---

[24] Short, J., Williams, E., & Christie, B. (1976). *The social psychology of telecommunication.* London: John Wiley; Parks, M. R., & Floyd, K. (1996). Making friends in cyberspace. *Journal of Communication, 46,* 80-97; Michailidis A., & Rada, R., (1997). Activities and communication modes. *International Journal of Human-Computer Studies, 46,* 469-483.

[25] Lea, M., & Spears, R. (1991). Computer-mediated communication, de-individuation and group decision-making. *International Journal of Man-Machine Studies, 34,* 283-301; Lea, M., & Spears, R. (1995). Love at first byte? Building personal relationships over computer networks. In J. T. Wood & S. Duck (Eds.), *Under-studied relationships: Off the beaten track* (pp. 197-233). Thousand Oaks, CA: Sage; Spears, R., & Lea, M. (1994). Panacea or panopticon?: The hidden power in computer-mediated communication. *Communication Research, 21,* 427-459; Walther, J. B. (1992). Interpersonal effects in computer-mediated interaction: A relational perspective. *Communication Research, 19,* 52-90; Walther, J. B. (1995). Relational aspects of computer-mediated communication: Experimental observations over time. *Organization Science, 6*(2)Signal delay effects on rapport in telepsychiatry. *Cyber Psychology and Behavior, 3,* 119-127; Nowak, K. L., Watt, J., Walther, J. B., Pascal, C., Hill, S., & Lynch, M. (2004, January). Contrasting time mode and sensory modality in the performance of computer mediated groups using asynchronous videoconferencing. *System Sciences,* 29-38.

[26] Champion, 1988; Parks & Floyd, 1996; Michailidis & Rada, 1997; Michailidis & Rada, 1997; McGrath, 1990; Hain, Chuan, Trever, & Detenber, 2004 (See eCounseling.com/static/board for full references)

modalities to be equal, and in some cases greater, than in-person services (see endnotes for a list of studies).[27]

Financial Viability

Financial issues include the cost of beginning and maintaining a practice; receiving training, marketing, acquiring clients, and receiving payment.[28] Currently, literature does not show clearly whether Online Counseling is advantageous or disadvantageous to counselor financial viability.

Text-based Online Counseling: The Plot Thickens

The Clinical Social Work Federation states in reference to text-based counseling, "... psychotherapy services cannot be delivered online [specifically via text] because of the inherent nature of the service and, therefore, the federation is opposed to the practice of Internet-based treatment."[29] However, others involved in the research and practice of online

---

[27] Barak & Wander Schwartz, 1999; Weinberg, Shmale, Uken, & Wessel, 1996; Lynch, Tamburring, & Nagel, 1997; Reese, Collie, & Brossart, 2002; Consumer Reports, 1995; Reese et al., 2000; Ben-Ari and Azaiza, 2001; Hornblow & Sloane, 1980; Celio, Winzelberg, Wilfley, Eppstein-Herald, Springer, & Taylor, 2000; Robinson & Serfaty, 2001; Winzelberg, Eppstein, Eldredge, Wilfley, Dasmahapatra, Dev, & Taylor, 2000; Zabinski, Pung, Wilfley, Eppstein, Winzellberg, Celio, & Taylor, 2001; Klein & Richards, 2001; Lange, Van de Ven, Schrieken, Bredeweg, & Emmelkamp, 2000; Stroem, Pattersson, & Andersson, 2000; Tate, Wing, & Winett, 2001 (See eCounseling.com/static/board for full references)

[28] Grohol, J. (1997). Why online psychotherapy? Because there is a need. Retrieved July 12, 2005, from http://psych-central.com/best/best4.htm; Slavich, S. (2003). *The status of online mental health services.* Unpublished doctoral dissertation, *Wichita State University. Wichita*; Gladding, S. T. (2004). *Counseling: A comprehensive profession. (5th ed.).* USA: Prentice Hall.

[29] Lonner, R. B., Trimm, S., Phillips, D. G., Amey, B., & Jean Synar, B. (2001). CSWF position paper on internet text-based therapy. *Clinical Social Work Federation.*

counseling disagree.[30] Proprietors of text-based counseling identify numerous intrinsic advantages to the modality—in addition to those of Online Counseling in general. These proposed advantages are described below.

Attention and Reflection

Text based interactions (especially those with a time delay) allow both client and counselor to pay close attention to their communication exchanges, and reflect on their own thoughts and feelings, while still in dialogue.[31]

Confession and Framing

A client's need to confess is automatically framed through the process of writing.[32] For example, journaling is sometimes assigned as homework to persons participating in in-person counseling, partly because of its framing and cathartic effects.

Objectivity and Externalization

Writing often invokes one to reread and review what was written, a process that promotes increased objectivity and externalization of a problem on the part of the client.[33]

---

[30] Fenichel, M. (2001, July 24). A Response to the Clinical Social Work Federation Position Paper on Internet Text-Based Therapy: A response from the president of ISMHO. Retrieved December 12, 2004, from http://ismho.org/issues/cswf.htm

[31] Suler, J. (2000). Psychotherapy in cyberspace: A 5-dimensional model of online and computer mediated psychotherapy. *CyberPsychology and Behavior, 3,* 151-160; Suler, 2004

[32] Speyer & Zack, 2003

[33] Childress, 2000

Associations and Insight

New associations, insights, and the recovery of old memories are common benefits of the process of writing out one's story. Further, it has been said that while with in-person sessions a client may speak for an hour and not reach the heart of a matter, with email Online Counseling a client can communicate more in *one sentence* written after an hour of reflection.[34]

Accountability

Text-based interactions allow participants to comment on and directly quote pertinent excerpts of previous exchanges. This heightens the accountability of both client and counselor to their statements.

Ownership and Control

Clients might communicate in a less restricted manner by text, for they are less affected by positive or negative leads of a therapist.[35] Clients also possess heightened ownership of the counseling process for they set the pace and tone by controlling both the frequency and content of disclosures.

Maximum Anonymity

While all Online Counseling methods increase client anonymity, text-based counseling offers more anonymity that even telephone counseling, for clients need not even share the timbre of their voice with a counselor.

Testament of Treatment Progress

Discussions are easily saved or printed with text counseling, allowing clients

---

[34] Speyer & Zack, 2003
[35] Suler, 2004

to reread therapeutic guidance years after the termination of therapy. This may strengthen old resolutions, and be a testament of the client's treatment progress.

The Debate Continues

The aim of this lesson was not to advocate for, or oppose, Online Counseling practices; it was simply to introduce the proposed advantages and disadvantages. Though it is difficult for me to hide some of my bias, I will denounce neither the pessimism nor the over-enthusiasm that exists in the field (though I may want to).

To do this would make me a politician either *for* or *against*—another voice of *opinion*, not of legitimate *conclusion*.

In order for authoritative assertions to be made, there are many meaningful studies that remain to be conducted on the various counseling factors, the proposed advantages and disadvantages mentioned. For now the debate continues. However, if good research, honest appraisals, legitimate concerns and open attitudes continue in the manner they have for the last several years, Online Counseling may soon stand as an accepted and invaluable tool to bring help and healing to persons with a spectrum of needs, in a variety of settings.

Table 1. Online Counseling may possess advantages in addition to convenience.

In-person counseling	Online Counseling (telephone or online)
Has proven to be effective over many years of research and study	New research shows Online Counseling to be effective, and sometimes more effective than in-person counseling
Has proven to be effective for building rapport/relationship between counselor and client	New research shows Online Counseling is effective for building rapport/relationship between counselor and client
A client has 45-50 minutes to tell his/her story	A client has unlimited amounts of time to detail his/her story by email
Persons are often seen by members of their community at the counseling office	Social stigma is eliminated
Clients can seek out the best counselor in their area	Clients can look outside their area for an excellent counselor
Client and counselor must show up during a designated time and at a designated location	Client and counselor do not meet at a designated place, and sometimes there is no designated time
Rates can be expensive, especially in	Clients benefit from lower overhead

urban areas	costs of counselors
Usually takes place during business hours: 9-5, Monday-Friday	Has potential for extended and flexible hours
Is difficult for the sick or immobile	Is accessible to homebound and ailing persons
There is risk of counselor sexual or social misconduct	There is less potential for counselor sexual or social misconduct
Are often client waiting lists	A counselor is always available
A counselor might not be experienced with the client's presenting problem	Clients can search for a counselor experienced with their problem issues
Counselor may not be knowledgeable of the client's ethnicity or language	Clients can select a counselor knowledgeable of their ethnicity and language
Client needs to overcome their apprehensions and fears of seeking counseling	Feeling more anonymous, clients with apprehensions and fears are more likely to seek counseling
Is ideal for clients who communicate well verbally	Is ideal for clients who communicate well verbally or by writing
Clients commit time to commuting, and often the "waiting room" experience	Client time is spent on counseling issues
Clients feel an empty space between sessions	With email, there is no "end" to a conversation, so clients feel continually

	in dialog with their counselor
Clients may be intimidated by the counselor	Clients are less likely to feel intimidated by the counselor
Clients may forget their feelings, resolutions, and commitments spoken in session	Clients are able to save writings regarding their feelings, resolutions, and commitments
Clients might forget a counselor's guidance and advice	Clients are able to save a counselor's guidance and advice, if it is in writing
Clients might not see clearly their progress	Saved text is a testament to a client's treatment progress

Lesson 47:
Online Counseling: Looking Back 12+ Years

How quickly things change, or do they? Issues of ethics, privacy, and client demand have been forefront topics since the inception of online therapy. In this lesson, I look at where Online Counseling was over half a decade ago, and note major changes to the present day. Then, with the risk of sounding like Ken Olson (Founder of Digital Equipment Corporation), who in 1977 said *"There is no reason anyone would want a computer in their home."* I'll make a few predictions about where Online Counseling might be going.

Ethics

A dozen years ago, if I would give a lecture about online therapy, I would spend the first half of the speech describing the debate over whether online and telephone therapy were legitimate clinical practice: *"Is it within the bounds of a therapy license?"* was the dominant question from the audience. The Clinical Social Work Federation, in 2001, had issued a statement denouncing text-based therapy, and around the same time the APA issued an, at best, neutral statement that *"The Ethics Code...has no rules prohibiting such services."*

Today, many persons at my lectures already provide some form of online care. Also, over the past seven years the ACA, NBCC, and other associations have added online counseling into their ethical codes (the AACC is planning the same as they revamp their ethics code this year). Therefore, I don't even address whether or not online therapy is legitimate practice; I focus on how to provide it ethically.

Privacy

Ten years ago, people were really, *really*, concerned about Internet security. Many seemed paranoid, certain that electronic data would jeopardize their privacy and increase their susceptibility to identify theft. They were right to be concerned.

Over the last several years, government agencies have lost personal information of U.S. citizens, including the Office of Inspector General at the U.S. Department of Transportation which, in 2006, lost a laptop containing data on 133,000 Florida residents. In March of 2008, 2,500 patients' personal health information (PHI) was lost by the National Institutes of Health (NIH). Not to be outdone, that same month, Hannaford and Sweetbay supermarkets lost 4.2 million customer credit card numbers to hackers—oops! There are hundreds, if not thousands, of stories like this; and some estimate that 1 in 5 persons in the U.S. has been a victim of identity theft.

Microsoft CEO Steve Ballmer, this month (July, 2009), described a huge need for cyber security, stating, *"The president needs to use his 'bully pulpit' to make sure businesses and local governments are protecting their data."* He explained *"information technology departments' vigilance has trended down over the past few years."*

A good sentiment, but it is unclear whether *vigilance* is enough. Today, a clinician can be vigilant 99 percent of the time, but one small error—connecting to the wrong wireless network, losing a USB flash drive, failing to log out of a program, or even forgetting to beta carbon copy an email can mean the PHI of hundreds, or hundreds of thousands, is compromised.

Expect to see more privacy disasters in the years to come.

Client Demand

Over the past 12 years we have learned a lot about client demand.

Online care is a tiny fraction of the counseling market. Also, in the current recession, private pay practices are hurting (Online Counseling practices are, in nearly 100 percent of cases, private pay). Hence, unless one is a fantastic marketer, has a huge fan base, or some really lucrative niche, a thriving online-only practice is not likely *Side note: Life coaches are similar. They usually work by telephone or online, but the most successful life coaches I know are the ones teaching life coaching, not providing it.*

Online Counseling has a place, as a minority prefers it to in-office care, and some clients opt for online care in addition to their in-office sessions. Successful therapists are using telephone and online care as a way to add value for their current clients. This, I predict, will continue to grow.

Lesson 48:
What Online Counseling won't do for Your Practice

Every week, for the past several years, I've received calls from counselors who've decided to begin offering online therapy. I used to respond to these calls with excitement: "Great! Congratulations! Welcome to the club!" I would say. However, more recently I've become a bit hesitant with my cheers, "wait a second" I might say, "What are you expecting to happen when you start offering online therapy?"

Too often, the counselor's response sounds something like this. "Well, I'm getting fewer new clients in my face-to-face practice, so I was thinking that online counseling would provide a much larger pool of potential clients." Then the counselor will ask me, "How long do you think it will take for me to have a full caseload?"

"Well, that's the thing," I'll say, "Caseloads of online clients don't just happen; they take a lot of effort to build. Being on the Internet isn't the solution to all your private practice woes."

And then, I will tell them what I'm about to tell you.

Online Counseling is a Small Pond

In the example above, the counselor is operating under an misconception—the syllogism is as follows:

- **Major Premise:** Big Nets Catch Fish
- **Minor Premise:** With Online Counseling, I Have a Big Net
- **Conclusion:** With Online Counseling, I Will Catch Fish

Brings you back to undergraduate philosophy, doesn't it? In less philosophical terms, the reasoning sounds like this: "There are millions of people online who want counseling. I should have no problem finding lots of clients!"

And here's the flaw. An online counselor's net may be huge, but the pond is small.

According to Google, in a recent month there were 1,220,000 web searches for the keyword "Counselor." In the same month, there were 6,600 searches for the keyword "Online Counselor."

Note huge difference: 1,213,400 more searches for "counselors", compared to "online counselors." Few clients are looking for online counseling (I wonder how many of those 6,600 searches were from counselors themselves!).

Other Nets in the Pond

When it comes to online counseling, there is more competition every day. While it is true that most counselors in the USA have no Internet presence what-so-ever, there are still thousands of therapists providing online services. In addition, the growing field of life coaching creates competition for counselors—and life coaches customarily provide services via telephone, or online.

Make no mistake, competition for online (and telephone) clients is strong, and any new online counselor is entering a competitive arena.

Immediate Benefits for Online Counselors

This lesson is not meant to discourage. All hope is not lost for the therapist considering online counseling! There are some immediate benefits to having an infrastructure for efficiently and ethically providing online counseling. Such will allow you to:

1. Retain some clients who relocate (a common problem in college towns like mine, Boston, MA)
2. Help clients who can't make it to all of their appointments (stuck at work, stuck in traffic, traveling, etc.)
3. Attract a small number of new clients (your net will catch some fish)

The Competitive Online Counselor

Build a Business

Going online is not an alternative to the arduous task of building a counseling business. Therapists need to develop a solid strategic plan. Develop a brand. Become a thought leader in the field. One even needs advertising and PR. For starters, I recommend that every aspiring online therapist should become an active part of the online communities where they are hanging their virtual shingle.

Find a Niche

Client X needs counseling. What makes you the best choice?

One way to attract online clients is to specialize. Focus your efforts on a specific type of client: clients with liver cancer, clients with pregnant teens, clients who have lost a child, desperate housewives, Americans living in Japan, Japanese living in the Americas...you get the picture.

People are more likely to try online counseling if they feel they will be able to talk with the expert in the exact area that they need help.

Remember...

Online counseling is not your niche! It is a method of delivering service. Don't just be online—be so valuable that people across the country are calling and emailing you to ask—"Do you see online clients?"

Lesson 49:
Dark: Why Online Counseling Practices Fail

Understanding the Keys to a Successful Online Counseling Practice

You're planning to offer online counseling. You've crunched the numbers and determined there are at least a billion people on the Internet. To be successful, you need to attract about 30 of them. This should be easy, right? **Maybe not.... Here's why.**

1. Most Clients Don't Want Online Counseling

A counselor interested in offering online counseling can list the benefits. A client:

1. Doesn't need to travel/commute to their session
2. Has a greater sense of safety and anonymity
3. Can participate from the comfort of home
4. And so on ...

The problem with this list is that these are attributes of online counseling that the counselor perceives as valuable. They are not, typically, solving a problem for the counselor's clients. No client has sat in their office and said, "This is okay, but man would this be better if I was at home on my couch."

Perhaps, rather than a keen sense of what the market wants, the above is a type of projection — they're benefits the counselor will enjoy: working from the comfort of home, etc.

At my practices' centralized contact center, we regularly get calls from potential clients located in areas where we don't have a convenient location. In these instances, we'll usually offer an online option.

The outcome: Even when someone has reached out specifically to our company, a strong majority of callers will decline the online offer and continue his/her search for someone he/she can literally "go see."
The fact is, counseling is an incredibly personal endeavor, and while tech-savvy consumers communicate with friends and family using Snapchat, WhatsApp and FaceTime, when confiding in a counselor it seems that most clients still want the in-person experience.

This might change. New ideas can take time to catch on.
Videoconference was widely available for a decade before people really began using it. There was a time in the 1990s when consumers rejected the concept of Clorox wipes because, "Why would anyone need that?" Today, paper towels pre-soaked in disinfectant is a huge business. As far as online counseling is concerned, the market has spoken ... for the moment.

2. The Problem of Money

While there are some exceptions, most third-party payers won't reimburse for online counseling (even during winter storm emergencies this year, we couldn't get private insurance companies to budge on this).

For insurance companies that do cover telehealth services, many still require the patient to report to an office to participate. **Did you catch that?** Here's an example: At our Richmond, Virginia, office, we can employ a psychiatrist from Alexandria, Virginia, and pipe him/her in via videoconference.

However, clients still need to come to the office for the session if they want their insurance to pay. Hence, online doesn't necessarily mean home-based.

3. State Licensure Lines

In the 90s and early 00s there was a debate related to the issue of "point-of-service", which refers to where an online counseling session actually takes place. Some argued that the point-of-service should be where the client resides, while others contended that it should be where the provider is delivering service. With the later, the client would figuratively travel on the "information superhighway" to exercise his/her right to solicit the services of an expert outside his/her state or providence.

I liked the, "where the provider resides" position. It made sense. The counselor would abide by the rules and regulations of his/her state of licensure, and wouldn't have to worry about from where their client was hailing. Alternatively, making the point of service where the client resides would shut down legitimate online providers but do nothing to stop unscrupulous unlicensed 'counselors' offering services on the web.

Unfortunately, according to most licensure boards the point of service has been determined to be where a client resides. Hence, even if you're practicing within your state of licensure, you better make sure your clients are also residing in your state.

Making it Work

Now that I've mentioned some reasons why online counseling practices struggle, here's how to beat the odds and make yours work.

1. Specialize

Instead of viewing online counseling as a "convenient" alternative to in-person sessions, consider it an inconvenience that some clients might be willing to make to seek your specific counsel. Earn this honor through thought leadership.

For example, a client is struggling after receiving a rejection letter from a college or grad school. You've written highly insightful and helpful articles on exactly that topic. After finding and reading your insights online, the client is willing to sacrifice an in-person connection with a local counselor to connect with you — someone he or she knows understands his/her disappointment and difficult situation.

2. Transition

While it's difficult to convert potential clients seeking counseling into online clients, it's much easier to transition in-person clients to online clients once a relationship has been established. Hence, if you have a caseload and you're looking to transplant yourself, you may find that most of your clients are willing to go online to continue your work together.

3. Snow Days

If you're in a northern state, consider introducing online counseling as an alternative to a day of cancelled sessions during a snow emergency. Of course, third-party payers still aren't likely to pay for online sessions. For insurance clients, consider accepting their usual co-pay as full payment for the session (sometimes a $25 co-pay is better than $0 for the hour).

4. Coaching

While you will need to proceed with extreme caution, for persons soliciting your services outside your state, while you (in most circumstances) won't be able to provide mental health counseling, you may be able to provide coaching.

With coaching, you can't diagnose or treat mental health issues, but you might be able to help with non-clinical life issues. Be sure to check with your licensure board and also have a very clear informed written consent process detailing the scope of the services you can provide in a coaching relationship.

Beating the Odds

Starting an online practice isn't easy. There are clinical, administrative and ethical implications of offering online services. Do your homework before hanging a virtual shingle.

Lesson 50:
How to Become an "Online Famous" Therapist

At a recent marketing convention, a keynote speaker addressed the audience. He said, "Everyone I meet wants to have the #1 website on Google, have the biggest and most responsive email list, and have the most followers on Twitter. Today, I have a surprise for you..." The speaker looked out over the crowd—there were 1000 people in attendance.

"I have placed a bright green card under one of your chairs. If you have that card, you will receive all those things today. Take a look, and whoever has the card, come up on stage and tell everyone why you deserve to have all these things." The speaker then waited a moment as the crowd started to shuffle and reach under their chairs. Then he said, "Ok I lied. There's no card, but you should have seen your faces! First TERRIFIED it was going to be you, and then smug, as if you were thinking to yourself 'I can't wait to hear what that poor sucker with the card is going to say.'"

The persons in the audience were nervous about the reward because, simply, they didn't *deserve* it. No one in the room was worthy of the things the "green card" was supposed to bring them. Hence, the number one rule of being online famous: you need to be worthy of that fame.

How to Become Worthy of Online Counseling Fame

How does the story above apply to online therapists? Very well, in fact. Here are a few things to keep in mind as you are promoting your therapy services online.

1) Find a Therapy Niche

Imagine the Internet as a loud, crowded room. As someone who wants to be seen by others, you need to stand out. You need to find a niche. Often I encounter people who think that "online counseling" is their niche. It's not. Online counseling (or telephone counseling) is simply the portal through which therapists provide their niche services.

Similarly, Christian therapy is too big to be a niche. Maybe if you are providing Christian therapy in an underserved area, you can be known as the town's local Christian therapist, but online there are thousands of Christian therapists, so you won't stand out. Need ideas? Here are some examples of niches: Christian Anorexia Specialist, Sports Psychology for X Games Athletes, Broken Heart Recovery Therapist.

Many therapists avoid niches, trying to make their area of focus as broad as possible. The hope: broad offerings will appeal to more people. This is not true online. The question of potential clients is often "why see a therapist by computer, if I can see one in my home city?" Answer: because the X Games athlete specialist is too far away to see in person, and that's the person who can help them the most.

2) Speak, speak, and speak some more

Once you decide on your niche (hopefully one in which you have a genuine competency), then it's time to speak on it, and speak on it, and speak on it some more. It's time to establish yourself as the quintessential professional on the topic.

Often times, a person will have great ambitions, but their enthusiasm wanes before they can see the fruit of their labors. An example of this would be someone who decides on a title for their blog, and then never writes anything; or someone who has a Facebook profile without so much as a personal photo uploaded.

Even if you are time-starved, you can still work toward being an online famous counselor. The general consensus is that a person can grow their online fame with an hour a day of contribution. Micro-blogging (i.e., Twitter.com) has made it easier to post frequently, because every post is limited to 140 characters. One of the great things about this format is that, if you don't have time to generate new content, it's completely acceptable to point people to other people's content on your topic. Matt drudge (Drudge Report) almost exclusively directs readers to content created by others, and he has one of the most visited websites on the web (give Matt Drudge the green card, and he'll tell you exactly why he deserves it—he broke the Monica Lewinski story in 1998, and now he updates the news on his web site every 3 minutes, 24/7/365. He posts top news stories, written by others, in a no-frills format).

3) Master the Online Tools

If you are serious about becoming famous online, you must become an expert with online social platforms. Buys books on Twitter, Facebook, Myspace, and any Blogging, Vlogging, or Web 2.0 application you might use. Attend seminars, webinars, and adult education classes. Spend time learning these tools and it will pay off.

I tell this to some counseling professionals and they say, "I'm not interested in all that. That's not what I want to do." They expect that their web developer can take care of "the technical side". But when it comes to online social networking, it doesn't work that way. You can't be ignorant to how things work, and expect to appear competent —not unless you hire someone to sit next to you and tell you *when* to post, *what* to title your post, *where* to tag it, *how* to bookmark it, *who* to syndicate it to, and so on. Just knowing about therapy isn't enough.

A final word of advice: As you move forward, I promise you will do a lot of things wrong, but you will do more things right. Just being online, communicating and interacting will lead people to your niche; in time, an hour a day will make you worthy of the online fame you're destined for!

Lesson 51:
Online Networking With Counseling Clients

WARNING: The landscape of online social networks, professional licensure boards' policies, and professional associations ethical codes regarding communication with clients through social networking websites is rapidly evolving. Rapid is an understatement, since I've written and revised this chapter a number of the websites that I mention don't even exist anytime (I left them in for nostalgia—how I miss some of them). Do check with your state's licensure board and your professional association's code of ethics before engaging in any connection with any client online. Below is my opinion, but my opinion might deviate from the opinion of the powers that govern your license to practice!

I have profiles on Youtube, Twitter, LinkedIn, Digg, Reddit, Technorati, Ning, Squidoo, XING, Yahoo Answers, Quora, Instagram, MySpace, G+, Yedda, Furl, Blogger, WordPress, StumbleUpon, del.icio.us, Yelp, Knol, Facebook, Orkut, Foursquare, Pinterest, Ello, and Skype… to name a few.

Most of these accounts I hardly use. Several I've been on once to create the account and only remember them when I receive email newsletters, which I unceremoniously delete. And, now that I'm thinking of it, a few of the above sites might be defunct by now.

Students and colleagues have been finding me online for several years, so I'm used to getting the occasional "friend request" from someone I have taught or worked with. However, more and more often I am receiving social networking requests from clients—either my own, or from clients of other providers at Thrive Boston Counseling. This poses some clinical and ethical considerations.

When I started receiving networking requests from clients, my initial reaction was to decline them. It's hard not to conclude that the wisest policy is to dissuade any online social networking (i.e., "Facebooking") between yourself and your clients. However, such connections may not be wrong per se, and might be justifiable under certain conditions.

Taking a look at my personal Facebook page, I have over six hundred friends—it's not an exclusive network. In fact, I use it for professional purposes as much as I do personal ones. And with that, my policy has been to accept almost all networking requests (excluding spammers and clients) without reservation. Hence, if I decline a client's request to join such a non-exclusive network, the question ensues, am I being too rigid? If the client realizes that I'll connect with anyone other than him/her, could that harm therapeutic rapport?

Approving a client as a "friend" on Facebook, or a connection on LinkedIn (the two places where I most often receive requests) will grant him access to mostly benign information: a few photos, links to articles I like, my status updates (which, since they are syndicated to over 600 'friends,' are benign), and some biographical information that is public anyhow, as I don't have that information set to private (i.e., anyone can go to www.facebook.com/anthonycentore and see my information)

However, approving the connection will also allow the client to see comments and photos of the students, colleagues, family, and 'friends' I have added prior. And this could blur professional boundaries, as well as spell disaster for psychoanalysts who prefer to be a blank slate for client projection.

Moreover, if the client is in anyway a dangerous person, increased access to my loved ones becomes risky, even downright scary. For all of these reasons, I have decided that I need a policy for any client who requests a "personal" online networking connection.

Online Networking Policy (an evolving draft)

If you are plugged into Online Social Networking, here are a few guidelines for handling connections and interactions with clients.

1) Never solicit a personal connection.

While it may be a stretch, a personal online connection could constitute a dual-relationship. According the ACA code of ethics (A.5.c. Nonprofessional Interactions or Relationships (Other Than Sexual or Romantic Interactions or Relationships)), "Counselor–client nonprofessional relationships with clients, former clients, their romantic partners, or their family members should be avoided, except when the interaction is potentially beneficial to the client." The code continues on to detail that therapists have a responsibility to document and justify why the nonprofessional relationship is taking place, and how it will be beneficial to the client.

Having a client connected with you on LinkedIn or Facebook probably isn't enough to constitute a full-blown nonprofessional interaction or relationship.

However, because it's a grey area, refraining from soliciting these connections is advisable.

Note: Soliciting clients to become "fans" of a professional / business page is different from a personal online networking connection, and would not constitute a dual role. In fact, when done correctly, having a business presence on Facebook (or other social networking sites) is a great way to add value for your clients, and promote your practice.

2) Discuss with the client his or her reasons for requesting a connection.

Irvin Yalom once wrote that if a client went to hug him at the end of a session, he would hug the client, but then talk about the meaning of the hug with them in the next appointment. Similarly, addressing client motivations for an online connection could be good "grist for the mill" in the therapy process.

Questions to consider: What is the client's motive to establish an online connection? Is it:

1. To learn more about who you are?
2. To read articles you are writing?
3. To have another method of contacting you for clinical or scheduling questions?
4. A friendly courtesy?
5. An attempt to use the counseling relationship as a friendship?
6. An attempt to become a part of your personal life?

Sometimes there is no motive! Social networking sites are often asking for permission to connect users to everyone in their email contact lists. Almost every week, I receive a networking request on Facebook or LinkedIn from someone who I don't know, and respond, "Hi, thanks for the networking request. Have we met in person?" The person responds that they were a client—or a potential client who never scheduled—of Thrive, and received the request because they solicited a connection with everyone in their email contact list.

3) Discuss risks and liabilities with the client.

Clients may not have considered the risks of being connected with you online. These risks vary depending on the client, but may include the following:

First, clients may underestimate the potential for negative emotions they might feel being in your network. For instance, perhaps clients have not considered what it will be like to see pictures of your friends and family—people who have a personal relationship with you; potentially one that your clients might desire.

Second, simply being in your network may compromise a client's confidentiality, as he/she is visible to your other connections. This risk is increased if the client comments on, tags, re-tweets, reposts, or "likes" content that you post. If others inquire as to whom this connection is, you (the counselor) may be unable to respond.

Third, the client might attempt to use the therapeutic relationship as a friendship, which could hinder a therapeutic goal of clients developing healthy relationships outside of counseling.

4) Address expectations with the client.

What purpose does the client believe the online connection will serve?

The client may have unspoken, misguided, expectations about the online connection that you cannot accommodate, such as:

- Will the client expect you to message with him online?
- Will the client expect you to view, post on, or comment on his page?
- Will the client expect you to never view or comment on his page?
- Does the client hope to be added to your "Top Friends" list (ok, this is a bit 2004)?

5) Clean up your profile.

Consider minimizing the risk of blurring professional-personal boundaries by making your account less personal. Some time ago, I decided this was a necessary endeavor: gone are some of the pictures of my sisters and me making faces at the camera. Gone is the survey that says my "superhero personality type" is the Green Goblin.

Many of my new social networking accounts are for Thriveworks, not me personally—which minimizes future conflicts. Once, I considered making two profiles for each website (one personal, one professional), but rejected the idea when I realized there is nothing to prevent my clients from soliciting a connection with the "wrong" profile.

6) Establish boundaries.

While having a client in your online network may be permissible, there are some things not to do. Don't solicit interactions, comment on their wall, or make a habit of "liking" their posts—it's the online equivalent of going up to clients in public and saying "Hi!" And, please, don't play Farmville with your clients!

Today, there is a client in my "friend request" pending list, in limbo, neither declined nor approved. I might approve him, but not before we talk about it.

Connect with me online!

Facebook (personal): Facebook.com/anthonycentore

Facebook (professional): Facebook.com/thriveworks

LinkedIn: Linkedin.com/in/anthonycentore

Twitter: Twitter.com/thriveworks

Lesson 52:
Words of Encouragement

It is the dream of many counselors to own and run their own private practices (as I wrote earlier "to be your own boss, and steer your own ship!"). It's unfortunate how few clinicians obtain that dream and goal with any level of financial success.

Until now, there has been a dearth of information about building a successful counseling practice. Why is this? I've presented presentations on building a counseling business to audiences at the American Counseling Association, and overwhelmingly the response I've heard is that counseling programs in the United Stated simply do not prepare their students to be successful in private practice. I hope this changes in the years to come.

In this course, we have reviewed the pros and cons of opening your own practice—the risks, costs, and the benefits! I also tried to provide you a roadmap, to help you and your practice get to a place where you are successful in our extremely competitive marketplace. As I wrote this work, I drew from my own experience, as well as the experiences of trusted and respected colleagues. My hope is that this work hasn't felt theoretical to you, but practical and instructional. I worked to pack every lesson with practical content that you can take, and execute.

I sincerely hope that you've enjoyed this course, and I hope that it will be helpful on your journey.

Should you have any questions, or wish to contact me or my team anytime, please feel free to do so. You can reach our offices at 1-855-4-THRIVE. Also, my email is Anthony@thriveworks.com.

Thriveworks Medical Credentialing

Medical Credentialing is the process of becoming affiliated with insurance companies so that you can accept third party reimbursement.

While important for the success of a clinical practice, for many health professionals, medical credentialing is an unwelcome distraction from providing quality care to their patients (It doesn't need to be!).

Today's Patients Want to Use their Insurance

While many years ago, counseling professionals considered medical credentialing an option, today it has become more necessary than ever for providers to be "networked" with insurance companies, as more patients in the USA have health insurance than ever before, and because patients desire (even demand) to use their health insurance when seeking out counseling services.

In addition, medical credentialing is becoming more important as health insurance plans are becoming broader in the scope of treatments that they cover. For example, mental health parity, and fewer restrictions on pre-existing conditions.

Insurance Panels are Getting Full and Closing!

Unfortunately, insurance panels (for providers) are becoming increasingly full — meaning the process of medical credentialing is becoming more difficult every day, as insurance companies close provider panels, and make the barrier for counselors, or any health professionals, higher and more difficult to climb.

Medical Credentialing Help

If you're looking for a medical credentialing service that can take the burden of credentialing off your shoulders, we can do that too. We'd love to talk with you about full-service medical credentialing that guarantees success. Please feel free to call us at 1-855-4-THRIVE (1-855-484-7483). Or visit us online at http://credentialing.com

601: Private Practice Forms

Introduction and Disclaimer

At Thriveworks, we often receive requests from counseling providers who are looking for private practice forms (informed consent, intakes, PHI releases, etc). Hence, we have provided a number of the most commonly requested forms below. We have used these exact forms in our charter counseling office, in Cambridge, Massachusetts.

Please note, that we don't warranty these documents, and you will want to check with your respective ethical boards and state laws before utilizing any part of the following documents.

SAMPLE INTAKE FORM / NEW CLIENT QUESTIONNAIRE

Welcome to Thriveworks! Thank you for taking a few minutes to fill out this form. The information you provide is confidential, and will be helpful for you and your counselor/life coach when you meet for the first time. If you have any questions, just ask!

Today's Date_____

Name _____ Age ____ Date of Birth ___/___/__

Address _____

                street   city   state   zip

Phone (Primary) _____ (Secondary)_____

Email (please print clearly) _

Ethnicity_____ Where did you grow up? _____

Education _____ Occupation _____ SSN _____

What is your religious background / involvement?

_____

Emergency contact person (name, relationship, phone, address).

_____

Closest Relationships (please list name, birth date, relationship, and whether they live with you)

Name	Birth Date	Relationship	Living with you?
_____	_____	_____	_____
_____	_____	_____	_____

Please describe your current living arrangement (Do you live with others?)

_____

Have you participated in any therapy before? Y___N___

If yes, when? _____ Reason _____

Are you, currently seeing a psychiatrist, therapist, or helper? Y___ N__

Have you or a family member ever been hospitalized for mental or emotional illness?
Y____ N____

If yes, please explain—dates, where, reason: _____

Substance abuse / addiction history? No _____ Yes (please explain)

_____

Legal History (arrests, prison, DWI, parking tickets?)

_____

Medical Information: Doctor's name and phone

_____

May we send your doctor a short note, letting him / her know you've come to see us? (we
do not release details other than your name, for referral purposes) Y___ N___

Are you on any medications? Y__N__ If so, what and why?

_____

How can we help? Please tell us in your own words what brings you here

today_____

_____

_____

What are your 2 most important goals for therapy?

1. _____

2. _____

Common problem/symptom checklist. Fill in: 0-none, 1-mild, 2-moderate, 3-severe.

__marriage	__divorce/separation	__alcohol/drugs	__God/faith
__pre-marital	__child custody	__other addictions	__church/ministry
__being single	__disabled	__grief/loss	__past hurts
__sexual issues	__work/career	__depression	__codependency
__family	__school/learning	__fear/anxiety	__intimacy
__children	__money/budgeting	__anger control	__communication
__parents	__aging/dependency	__loneliness	__self-esteem
__in-laws	__weight control	__mood swings	__stress control

Family Information:

Marital Status (check any that apply):

Single ___ Dating ___ Committed relationship ___ Engaged ___

Married __ (how long? _____) Separated __ (how long? _____) Divorced __ (how long?_____)

Spouse's Name (if applicable) _____ Age _____ Occupation _____

I would describe my friendships as: Close __ Somewhat close___ Distant___ Conflicted___

I would describe my relationship with my mother as:

Close __ Somewhat close___ Distant___ Conflicted___

I would describe my relationship with my father as:

Close __ Somewhat close___ Distant___ Conflicted___

How many siblings do you have? _____

How would you describe your relationship? _____

Crisis Information: Are you having any current suicidal thoughts, feelings or actions?

Y_____ N_____

If yes, explain _____

Any current homicidal or violent thoughts or feelings, or anger-control problems?
Y____ N____

    If yes, explain _____

Any issues, hospitalizations, or imprisonments for suicidal or assault behavior?
Y_____ N____

    If yes, describe _____

Any current threats of significant loss or harm (illness, divorce, custody, job loss, etc.)?
Y___ N__

    If yes, describe _____

Who referred you to us? _____

THANK YOU for taking the time to fill out this information sheet. This will be reviewed with you during your first counseling / life coaching session.

SAMPLE CONSENT AND SERVICE AGREEMENT

Welcome to your first session at Thriveworks! This form provides information about our services: Please review it carefully, and feel free to ask us any questions!

Our Goal

It's our goal to offer a positive, empowering, and life-enriching experience for our clients.

About our Services

The potential benefits of counseling are many and include improved personal functioning, relationships, self-image, mood, and the attainment of personal goals. However, in some cases persons have reported feeling worse after counseling. Clients understand that healing and growth is difficult, and some discomfort will likely be a part of the counseling process.

Confidentiality

All communications and records with your counselor are held in strict confidence. Information may be released, in accordance with state law, when (1) the client signs a written release indicating consent to release; (2) the client expresses serious intent to harm self or someone else; (3) there is reasonable suspicion of abuse against a minor, elderly person, or dependent adult; (4) to acquire payment for services or for billing purposes; or (5) a subpoena or court order is received directing the disclosure of information. To protect your privacy to the greatest extent of the law, it is our policy to assert either (a) privileged communication in the event of #5 or (b) the right to consult with clients, if at all possible, before mandated disclosure in the event of #2 or #3.

Electronic Communication. Telephone and email are not encrypted methods of communication, and some confidentiality risk exists with their use. Counselors at Thrive sometimes communicate using these mediums. If you would prefer to not be contacted by telephone or email, please inform your counselor and we will honor this request.

Client Follow Up. Your counselor may follow up with you after counseling has ended. 1 month, 3 month, and 6 month follow up calls help us to see if gains made in counseling have been maintained. In addition, someone from our team might call you to ask for your feedback on your experience at Thriveworks. If you would prefer not to be contacted, simply inform your counselor and your preferences will be respected.

Scheduling and Cancellations

Scheduling an appointment is a commitment that both counselors and clients honor. Appointments can be cancelled or rescheduled if 48 hours' notice is provided. If sessions are cancelled or rescheduled with less than the required notice, or if a client misses a session, the client agrees to pay for that session (insurance will not pay for missed appointments). Please know that exceptions to this policy may be made in the instance of a serious medical emergency.

Conflicts

We work hard to ensure that you have a positive experience with us. However, if a conflict occurs, it is agreed that any disputes shall be negotiated directly between the parties. If these negotiations are not satisfactory, then the parties _agree_ to mediate any differences with a third-party mediator. If these are unsatisfactory, then the parties shall move to arbitration, and then binding arbitration, choosing a mutually agreeable arbitrator. Litigation shall be considered only if all of these methods of resolution are given a good faith effort and are unsatisfactory.

Emergency Contacts

Your counselor will establish emergency contacts for you, such as the phone number and location of a family member. Your counselor will also obtain alternative methods for contacting you, such as a mobile phone, or work phone number. These emergency contacts may be used if your counselor perceives a need. If you are in crisis and cannot reach your counselor, please go to your nearest emergency room.

Service Fees

Payment is due at the time of your scheduled session, and will be billed to your credit/bank card on file **(Note: Counselors do not accept money directly from clients)**. Any insurance co-pays or deductibles are due at the time of the session. Unfortunately, we cannot extend credit or provide services until payment is made. *Clients understand they are fully responsible for all fees if insurance or other vendor does not pay for any reason.*

We, the counselor and client, have read and fully understand and agree to honor this agreement.

Client(s) _____Date_____

Provider _____Date_____

SAMPLE RECEIPT FOR SERVICES

This receipt is to certify that (Client Name) _____ participated in counseling with (Therapist Name) _____ at *Thrive Counseling LLC* on (dates):

Counseling fees total _____. Admin fees total _____. Grand total _____. Paid in Full.

Procedural Code (ex: 90806, etc.) _____Diagnosis Code

_____

Tax ID of Thrive Counseling LLC is 26-3447487. For any additional confirmation or information, contact *Thriveworks* at 1-855-4-THRIVE, or via email at support@thriveworks.com

SAMPLE RELEASE OF MEDICAL RECORDS

Patient Authorization for Disclosure of PHI (Personal Health Information)

I, _____, wish to obtain a copy of my medical records.

Reason I am requesting my records:

_____

_____

___

I would like my records sent to:

_____

_____

___

I would like the following released:

_____ **Dates and charges of service.**

_____ **A summary of my sessions and treatment.**

_____ **My entire record.**

_____ **Other (explain)**

_____

Social Security Number: _____

Date of Birth: _____

Phone Number: _____

I understand that if I have any questions about my clinical records, or the content within, I can contact Thrive Counseling and someone will meet with me to discuss my records.

I understand that my treatment records are protected under the Health Insurance Portability and Accountability Act of 1996 ('HIPAA'), 45 CFR, Parts 160 & 164 and cannot be disclosed without my written consent unless otherwise provided for in the regulations. I also understand that I may revoke this consent at any time and that that any notice to revoke consent must be in writing.

Signature: _____   *Date:* _____

HIPAA: Sample Business Associate Agreement

Below is a sample Business Associate Agreement, in compliance with the HIPAA Omnibus rules for 2013.

Apparently, the new rules state that if person A has a business associate agreement with person B, and person B works with a 3rd party (person C) who might have access to the PHI, person B needs to issue a BAA to person C, and so on!!

Someday it's going to go full circle and someone's going to be issued a Business Associate Agreement (from person Z?), about their own PHI. Anyway, in the sample agreement there are some options for the user to adjust the agreement to fit their needs, without invalidating it or bringing it out of compliance.

We hope this helps!!
–Your Friends at Thriveworks

Sample Business Associate Agreement Provisions

*****NOTE: Words or phrases contained in brackets are intended as either optional language or as instructions to the users of these sample provisions.*****

Definitions

Catch-all definition:

The following terms used in this Agreement shall have the same meaning as those terms in the HIPAA Rules: Breach, Data Aggregation, Designated

Record Set, Disclosure, Health Care Operations, Individual, Minimum Necessary, Notice of Privacy Practices, Protected Health Information, Required By Law, Secretary, Security Incident, Subcontractor, Unsecured Protected Health Information, and Use.

Specific definitions:

(a) Business Associate. "Business Associate" shall generally have the same meaning as the term "business associate" at 45 CFR 160.103, and in reference to the party to this agreement, shall mean [Insert Name of Business Associate].

(b) Covered Entity. "Covered Entity" shall generally have the same meaning as the term "covered entity" at 45 CFR 160.103, and in reference to the party to this agreement, shall mean [Insert Name of Covered Entity].

(c) HIPAA Rules. "HIPAA Rules" shall mean the Privacy, Security, Breach Notification, and Enforcement Rules at 45 CFR Part 160 and Part 164.

Obligations and Activities of Business Associate

Business Associate agrees to:

(a) Not use or disclose protected health information other than as permitted or required by the Agreement or as required by law;

(b) Use appropriate safeguards, and comply with Subpart C of 45 CFR Part 164 with respect to electronic protected health information, to prevent use or disclosure of protected health information other than as provided for by the Agreement;

(c) Report to covered entity any use or disclosure of protected health information not provided for by the Agreement of which it becomes aware, including breaches of unsecured protected health information as required at 45 CFR 164.410, and any security incident of which it becomes aware; [The parties may wish to add additional specificity regarding the breach notification obligations of the business associate, such as a stricter timeframe for the business associate to report a potential breach to the covered entity and/or whether the business associate will handle breach notifications to individuals, the HHS Office for Civil Rights (OCR), and potentially the media, on behalf of the covered entity.]

(d) In accordance with 45 CFR 164.502(e)(1)(ii) and 164.308(b)(2), if applicable, ensure that any subcontractors that create, receive, maintain, or transmit protected health information on behalf of the business associate agree to the same restrictions, conditions, and requirements that apply to the business associate with respect to such information;

(e) Make available protected health information in a designated record set to the [Choose either "covered entity" or "individual or the individual's designee"] as necessary to satisfy covered entity's obligations under 45 CFR 164.524;
[The parties may wish to add additional specificity regarding how the business associate will respond to a request for access that the business associate receives directly from the individual (such as whether and in what time and manner a business associate is to provide the requested access or whether the business associate will forward the individual's request to the

covered entity to fulfill) and the timeframe for the business associate to provide the information to the covered entity.]

(f) Make any amendment(s) to protected health information in a designated record set as directed or agreed to by the covered entity pursuant to 45 CFR 164.526, or take other measures as necessary to satisfy covered entity's obligations under 45 CFR 164.526;

[The parties may wish to add additional specificity regarding how the business associate will respond to a request for amendment that the business associate receives directly from the individual (such as whether and in what time and manner a business associate is to act on the request for amendment or whether the business associate will forward the individual's request to the covered entity) and the timeframe for the business associate to incorporate any amendments to the information in the designated record set.]

(g) Maintain and make available the information required to provide an accounting of disclosures to the [Choose either "covered entity" or "individual"] as necessary to satisfy covered entity's obligations under 45 CFR 164.528;

[The parties may wish to add additional specificity regarding how the business associate will respond to a request for an accounting of disclosures that the business associate receives directly from the individual (such as whether and in what time and manner the business associate is to provide the accounting of disclosures to the individual or whether the business associate will forward the request to the covered entity) and the timeframe for the business associate to provide information to the covered entity.]

(h) To the extent the business associate is to carry out one or more of covered entity's obligation(s) under Subpart E of 45 CFR Part 164, comply with the requirements of Subpart E that apply to the covered entity in the performance of such obligation(s); and

(i) Make its internal practices, books, and records available to the Secretary for purposes of determining compliance with the HIPAA Rules.

Permitted Uses and Disclosures by Business Associate

(a) Business associate may only use or disclose protected health information [Option 1 – Provide a specific list of permissible purposes.] [Option 2 – Reference an underlying service agreement, such as "as necessary to perform the services set forth in Service Agreement."] [In addition to other permissible purposes, the parties should specify whether the business associate is authorized to use protected health information to de-identify the information in accordance with 45 CFR 164.514(a)-(c). The parties also may wish to specify the manner in which the business associate will de-identify the information and the permitted uses and disclosures by the business associate of the de-identified information.]

(b) Business associate may use or disclose protected health information as required by law.

(c) Business associate agrees to make uses and disclosures and requests for protected health information

[Option 1] consistent with covered entity's minimum necessary policies and procedures.

[Option 2] subject to the following minimum necessary requirements: [Include specific minimum necessary provisions that are consistent with the covered entity's minimum necessary policies and procedures.]

(d) Business associate may not use or disclose protected health information in a manner that would violate Subpart E of 45 CFR Part 164 if done by covered entity [if the Agreement permits the business associate to use or disclose protected health information for its own management and administration and legal responsibilities or for data aggregation services as set forth in optional provisions (e), (f), or (g) below, then add ", except for the specific uses and disclosures set forth below."]

(e) [Optional] Business associate may use protected health information for the proper management and administration of the business associate or to carry out the legal responsibilities of the business associate.

(f) [Optional] Business associate may disclose protected health information for the proper management and administration of business associate or to carry out the legal responsibilities of the business associate, provided the disclosures are required by law, or business associate obtains reasonable assurances from the person to whom the information is disclosed that the information will remain confidential and used or further disclosed only as required by law or for the purposes for which it was disclosed to the person, and the person notifies business associate of any instances of which it is aware in which the confidentiality of the information has been breached.

(g) [Optional] Business associate may provide data aggregation services relating to the health care operations of the covered entity.

Provisions for Covered Entity to Inform Business Associate of Privacy Practices and Restrictions

(a) [Optional] Covered entity shall notify business associate of any limitation(s) in the notice of privacy practices of covered entity under 45 CFR 164.520, to the extent that such limitation may affect business associate's use or disclosure of protected health information.

(b) [Optional] Covered entity shall notify business associate of any changes in, or revocation of, the permission by an individual to use or disclose his or her protected health information, to the extent that such changes may affect business associate's use or disclosure of protected health information.

(c) [Optional] Covered entity shall notify business associate of any restriction on the use or disclosure of protected health information that covered entity has agreed to or is required to abide by under 45 CFR 164.522, to the extent that such restriction may affect business associate's use or disclosure of protected health information.

Permissible Requests by Covered Entity

[Optional] Covered entity shall not request business associate to use or disclose protected health information in any manner that would not be permissible under Subpart E of 45 CFR Part 164 if done by covered entity. [Include an exception if the business associate will use or disclose protected health information for, and the agreement includes provisions for, data aggregation or management and administration and legal responsibilities of the business associate.]

Term and Termination

(a) Term. The Term of this Agreement shall be effective as of [Insert effective date], and shall terminate on [Insert termination date or event] or on the date covered entity terminates for cause as authorized in paragraph (b) of this Section, whichever is sooner.

(b) Termination for Cause. Business associate authorizes termination of this Agreement by covered entity, if covered entity determines business associate has violated a material term of the Agreement [and business associate has not cured the breach or ended the violation within the time specified by covered entity]. [Bracketed language may be added if the covered entity wishes to provide the business associate with an opportunity to cure a violation or breach of the contract before termination for cause.]

(c) Obligations of Business Associate Upon Termination.
[Option 1 – if the business associate is to return or destroy all protected health information upon termination of the agreement]

Upon termination of this Agreement for any reason, business associate shall return to covered entity [or, if agreed to by covered entity, destroy] all protected health information received from covered entity, or created, maintained, or received by business associate on behalf of covered entity, that the business associate still maintains in any form. Business associate shall retain no copies of the protected health information.

[Option 2—if the agreement authorizes the business associate to use or disclose protected health information for its own management and administration or to carry out its legal responsibilities and the business associate needs to retain protected health information for such purposes after termination of the agreement]

Upon termination of this Agreement for any reason, business associate, with respect to protected health information received from covered entity, or created, maintained, or received by business associate on behalf of covered entity, shall:

1. Retain only that protected health information which is necessary for business associate to continue its proper management and administration or to carry out its legal responsibilities;

2. Return to covered entity [or, if agreed to by covered entity, destroy] the remaining protected health information that the business associate still maintains in any form;

3. Continue to use appropriate safeguards and comply with Subpart C of 45 CFR Part 164 with respect to electronic protected health information to prevent use or disclosure of the protected health information, other than as provided for in this Section, for as long as business associate retains the protected health information;

4. Not use or disclose the protected health information retained by business associate other than for the purposes for which such protected health information was retained and subject to the same conditions set out at [Insert section number related to paragraphs (e)

and (f) above under "Permitted Uses and Disclosures By Business Associate"] which applied prior to termination; and

5. Return to covered entity [or, if agreed to by covered entity, destroy] the protected health information retained by business associate when it is no longer needed by business associate for its proper management and administration or to carry out its legal responsibilities.

[The agreement also could provide that the business associate will transmit the protected health information to another business associate of the covered entity at termination, and/or could add terms regarding a business associate's obligations to obtain or ensure the destruction of protected health information created, received, or maintained by subcontractors.]

(d) Survival. The obligations of business associate under this Section shall survive the termination of this Agreement.

Miscellaneous [Optional]

(a) [Optional] Regulatory References. A reference in this Agreement to a section in the HIPAA Rules means the section as in effect or as amended.

(b) [Optional] Amendment. The Parties agree to take such action as is necessary to amend this Agreement from time to time as is necessary for compliance with the requirements of the HIPAA Rules and any other applicable law.

(c) [Optional] Interpretation. Any ambiguity in this Agreement shall be interpreted to permit compliance with the HIPAA Rules.

Name_____

Signature_____ Date_____

Made in the USA
Columbia, SC
12 December 2017